Gao Xingjian

Ink Paintings by

Gao Xingjian

Nobel Prize Winner

Homa & Sekey Books
Dumont, New Jersey

FIRST AMERICAN EDITION

ISBN: 1-931907-03-X
Library of Congress Control Number: 2002101974

Publishers Cataloging-in-Publication Data

Ink Paintings by Gao Xingjian, Nobel Prize Winner
By Gao Xingjian

1. Painting, Chinese
2. Painter—China
3. Expatriate painter—Europe—France

I. Title ND1045. O128A 2002 759.951-dc21

Published by Homa & Sekey Books
138 Veterans Plaza
P. O. Box 103
Dumont, NJ 07628
Tel: (201)384-6692
Fax: (201)384-6055
Email: info@homabooks.com
Website: www.homabooks.com

Editor: Shawn X. Ye
Front Cover Art: Anxiousness (detail), 1986, 33.10 x 59.65 inches

Published by arrangement with modo Verlag GmbH, Freiburg, Germany
Printed in Germany
1 3 5 7 9 10 8 6 4 2

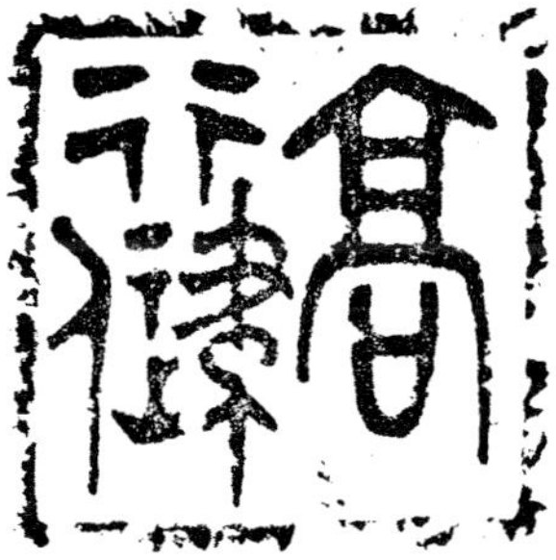
高行健

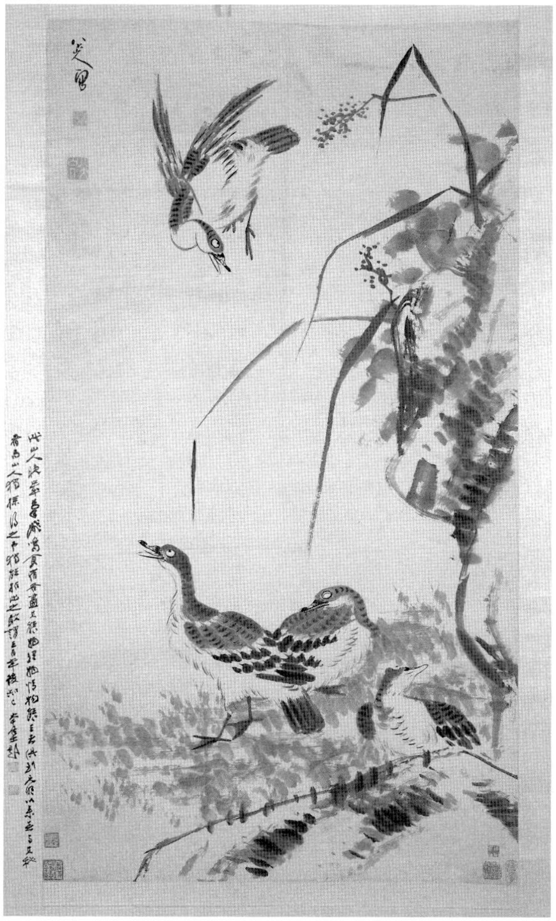

Wild Duck, 49.70 x 26.80 in
By Bada Shanren (Zhu Da) (1624 - 1705)
Morat Collection, Freiburg, Germany

Thoughts on Painting

Gao Xingjian

Following the realization of the possibilities of painting by Picasso and Kandinsky, abstract painting has wallowed for nearly a century. The question thus arises, what more can the realm of painting possibly produce? Following the supplanting of painting with collage, color, materials, photographic techniques, computer graphics, photoelectric techniques, text, and even conceptual games, can we continue on painting? Today, painting has come full circle to figurative painting. Confronting face-to-face the previous generations throughout its history, can painting today come up with any new performances?

Can painting escape the limitations of two dimensions and continue to be painting? Or perhaps we should ask: Without leaving the planar surface, can it find new possibilities in the treatment of space within these limitations? Further, within the restrictions of two dimensions, apart from points, lines, fields, colors, chiaroscuro, and arrangement, are there any other methods left? Or, perhaps to beg the question further: If the methods currently at our disposal are discarded, can painting still be considered painting? Going yet another step further, it can be asked whether after all these methods are taken away, the materials or colors which make up a plain surface themselves can be considered painting? Or maybe if actions are performed onto this surface, such as making a gash with a knife, ripping, or burning, or rolling over it with one's body, or letting a slug slime over it... can these be considered methods of painting?

Shall the constant promotion of the revolutionizing or reformation of "modernism" over the past century inevitably lead to the repudiation of this art? What exactly is "modernism"? Does it have any definite historical connotations? or is the transcendence of the era or the moment the one and only basis on which the value of art is judged? What does painting seek to express, and what is painting? Is its significance in the act of painting itself, or in its expression? Such questions confuse me. Not getting the answers, I have simply returned to two-dimensional surfaces and the traditional materials of rice paper, brush, and ink. And in so doing, I have discovered that painting with these materials holds endless delight. Furthermore, I realized that it is similar to writing, where even today in using the language of our forebears, we can still speak our own minds and come up with fresh things to say. Naturally, we can still come up with new paintings with the same old tools – the only question is how the artist re-familiarizes himself with the techniques used over and over by mankind since the inception of painting in civilization. There are two approaches to creating paintings on two-dimensional surfaces. First is realistic space, such as aligned perspective, to create the illusion of a third dimension. The other approach is recognizing the planar surface of painting, stressing the qualities of painting and painting directly on the surface. Both of these approaches can claim their own respective history and tradition in the East and West. However, the East and West seem to have switched roles and taken opposite paths in the modern painting. Since Cezanne, the efforts of Western painters have returned to the planar nature of painting, while Eastern painters have searched for depth on the planar surface. Each accomplished painter can be said to have found a certain resolution, while each artist who desires to make his or her creative mark on painting is faced with exactly such a dilemma.

For the painter, this space is not speculation; rather, one must accurately reflect one's treatment of space on the canvas or paper. This challenge is the final dividing line between wisdom and physical dexterity. That art is more than just empty talk is proven on the surface of a painting. Modern artists have found a number of ways to get around this problem, as with Picasso's division of cubes into planes, Cezanne's elimination of depth, Matisse's employment of strong color contrasts, Kandinsky's overlapping alignment, and the juxtaposition of real and imagined spaces. Zao Wou-Ki, who is after all Oriental, is just the opposite – applying layer upon layer of thin color in search of a depth not found in traditional Eastern painting. The so-called language of painting must be expressed by some type of method; otherwise, for the artist it is nothing more than empty talk. As for my own painting, naturally I intend to find my own solution. Perhaps, because I am after all still Chinese, I am accustomed to the free expression on two-dimensional surfaces in traditional Chinese painting, while the depth of Western painting has always been especially appealing to me. Consequently, even if I am using ink for free expression I look for this depth of space, albeit one which differs from Western perspective. There is a component of modern Chinese painting theory called "diffuse point perspective," which borrows Western art theory to interpret traditional Chinese painting – something which naturally makes sense.

By setting out from traditional Chinese freehand painting and attempting to achieve a depth of space, I am not coming from observation of actual depth of field, but rather depth which is visualized from within; it seems to have a feeling of perspective, but does not agree with perspective with a focus, and it is not poli-focal. When one maintains a certain inner vision, one finds that so-called 'distance' shifts and floats, much like a camera shooting in the dark whose auto-focus lens moves in and out in a herky-jerky fashion. This is merely a simple comparison, as when one closes one's eyes and views these images of the mind that appear at times, they are there before one's eyes but have no clear distance – not following the law of smaller objects further away and larger objects closer. How to capture such inner visions in the picture, yet without resorting to strict perspective, is the challenge I seek to resolve.

For my current purposes, I shall call this feeling of depth in inner visions "false perspective," and treat inner visions as different levels and different viewing angles. However, I shall place them in what seems like the same space, using different levels of space to create a feeling of perspective and compose an overall picture (rather than separate parts). This is a space conceived at will on the spur of the moment, not according to rules of perspective, and without particular focus or diffuse focus – yet still creating depth of field as if shot by a real camera. However, rather than objects or scenes, shadows are described – revealing themselves in the mind in unexpected places. Although the tangible feeling they have is illusory, such visions can definitely be achieved. All painting attempts to do is to turn the seeds of these visions into pictures.

Although these visions sometimes have colors, as they flash by in an instant they are difficult to grasp, making them murky. This is why expressing them with ink is closer, and why I only use monochromatic ink and not colors.

I first began painting abstract paintings with ink, as the brushing and spread of ink on rice paper in Chinese ink painting holds a definite kind of enjoyment and interest. My earliest abstract inks came from Zen paintings, where I sought not images but states of mind. Still, I hope that what is left on the paper can be made out as pictures after some time.

The ink left on the paper by the masters of traditional Chinese ink paintings is full of inexhaustible interest itself. Kandinsky's studies of points, fields, and lines did not mean removing the pure form of implication, which has its similarities to the spirit which is sought after in traditional Chinese ink painting. There, brush strokes and ink marks are not merely means to create forms, but their implications are equally important. My abstract ink paintings are not only imbued with a certain kind of form, but at the same time intend to let brush strokes and ink marks carry feeling and implication.

I gradually came to realize that the dividing line between the abstract and the figurative is not necessarily cut and dry, and that for me such a dividing line is increasingly unnecessary. As a result, some people see figurative images in my works, while others might see abstraction; it is images and forms at the same time. This is that quality of painting for which I strive – contained within the brush and ink, but also existing beyond them. Points, lines, and fields must contain the feeling of the brush and ink, and must in themselves form pictures. So for me, the dividing line between the figurative and the abstract is unimportant, which allows me to work spontaneously without any constraints.

When it comes to painting, I ascribe to no conceptual doctrines and belong to no school. The thing I fear most is the attachment of some new fashionable label to my work. I believe that the most important thing for an artist is to stay as far away from others as possible in order to avoid getting mixed up in some trend. If one is able to find one's own distinctive artistic expression, there can be no greater reward or joy. The reason is that, in real life, individual freedoms are invariably subject to constraints, and only in the realm of individual artistic creation can one achieve the freedom to truly express oneself. Yet this freedom depends on whether or not one can find the necessary form of expression, without which freedom of artistic expression is meaningless.

For the artist, freedom of artistic expression, more than the strict will, lies in the ease with which one employs one's chosen devices to achieve this freedom. This means that in addition to having (or not having) one's own thoughts, the artist must study the materials and tools he or she uses to see how much freedom can be achieved. Specifically, how else can the paper, brush, and ink be employed in ink painting? This depends on the investigation of the performance of materials and techniques of application. The more I investigate, the more I discover that the potential of ink painting is far from being exhausted, even though this art form has been around for at least 1,000 years. This art is expressed differently in the hands of each individual artist, which is also why ink painting is continually invested with new life. So I'm perfectly happy to keep working away in the realm of ink painting.

Actually the same is essentially true of oil painting. Nobody can say for sure when oil painting will be unable to come up with anything that was not painted previously. Granted, nowadays any material or techniques can be used in art, including computers and lasers, but I'm perfectly willing to manipulate monochromatic variation of depth with ink and paper within the bounds of two-dimensional surface to create my pictures. Broadly speaking, any kind of art is about striving for limitlessness under given restricted conditions.

What should art express? There is a different answer for each different artist, and exactly because of the different answers do we have a variety of artistic pursuits. Moreover, no answer is universal, or the only correct answer. In art, there is no judgment of right or wrong, or morality, because artists do not accept other people's truths. Because there is neither god nor master in art, artists are free to throw themselves into their endless pursuit and never notice how hard it is.

At the same time I adhere to the possibilities and interest of the ink and brush, I search for textural quality not found in traditional ink painting in an attempt to fuse the grace of ink painting with emotional quality expressed in oil painting. Not only do I place particular emphasis on the effects of ink saturation, but I also employ this to give images a different textural quality. Therefore, Ink is applied in several layers, creating contrasting image effects. Abstraction and concreteness become apparent from the composition of the work as well as from the contrast of the images. I also use light to enrich the expressive power of ink. My particular angle is that I do not set the source of light, unlike many Western paintings. I believe that light can be wherever there is life or spirit. When a person looks inside to see a vision, the image or the image's border emits a lustrous light, an effect created where ink meets ink.

Having also studied photography, I bring the viewing angle, depth of field, and focus of photography into my ink painting to look into the images of the mind, naturally resulting in images that cannot be captured with a camera. Art attempts to reach a realm that is unattainable in reality. Otherwise, why go through all the trouble?

I always listen to music while painting, waiting for the music to strike a chord in my heart before setting out. Once moved, images flow from me, and with the movement of the brush and ink, the music gives my painting a certain kind of rhythm. Music gives the respective components of painting (points, fields, and lines, or brush strokes) even more feeling, so why not use it? This method of creating shapes and images allows the various colors of mood, giving a painting a living presence.

I do not consider painting a pure expression of form. Form is admittedly important, especially in the plastic arts, where one cannot achieve expression without it. However, modern painting in this century has progressively approached purity of form, making pursuit of form into the ultimate aim of painting. Pure form, which is constantly losing expressiveness, has become increasingly close to decoration, to the extent that it has become a white wall, or a field of oils, a few blocks of color, or several lines, which is signed by the executor. This is the result of fruitless play with form, yet art has not been destroyed because of it.

If the self-expression of an artist becomes the direct expression of self, then one's art will be a mess. As the self (or ego) is a chaotic mass, or a black hole to begin with, unless an artist exercises self-knowledge and removes himself for dispassionate observation of the world (including the self), then what is there to see?

More than self-expression I see art as a case of self-purification – observing with a pair of somewhat sober eyes the ever-changing world and one's own mainly unconnected self. And although he may not understand the riddles of life, the artist can leave behind a surprise or two.

Paris, 14 July 1995

Paintings

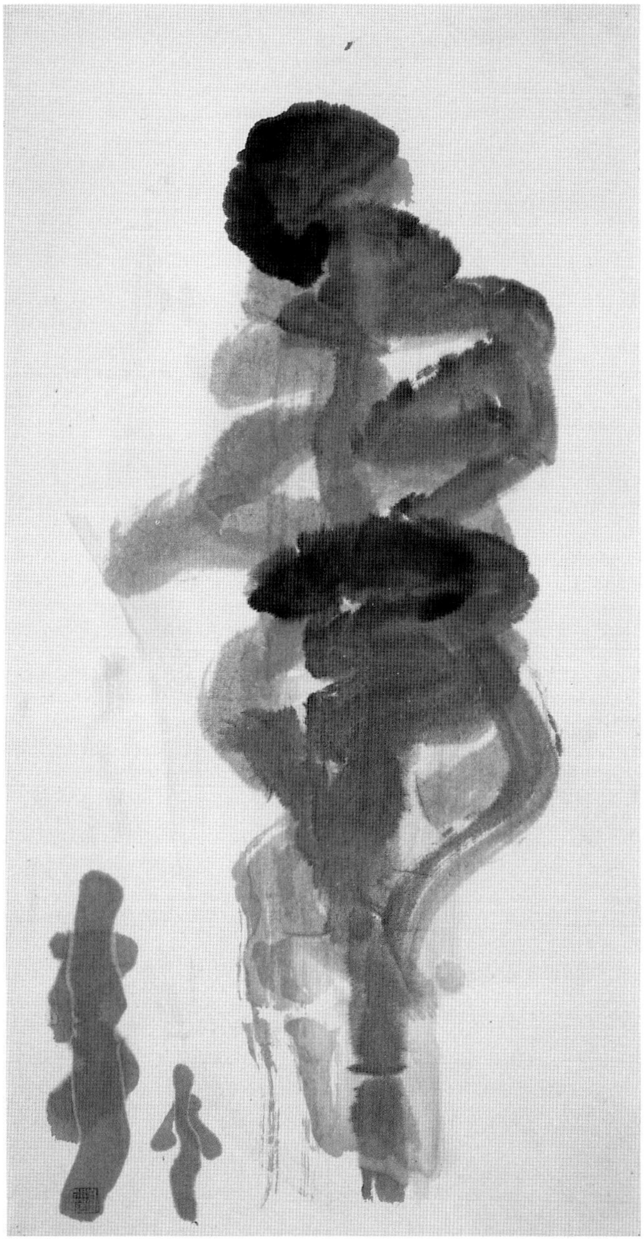

 The Soul of the Tree, 1983, 40.20 x 20.80 in

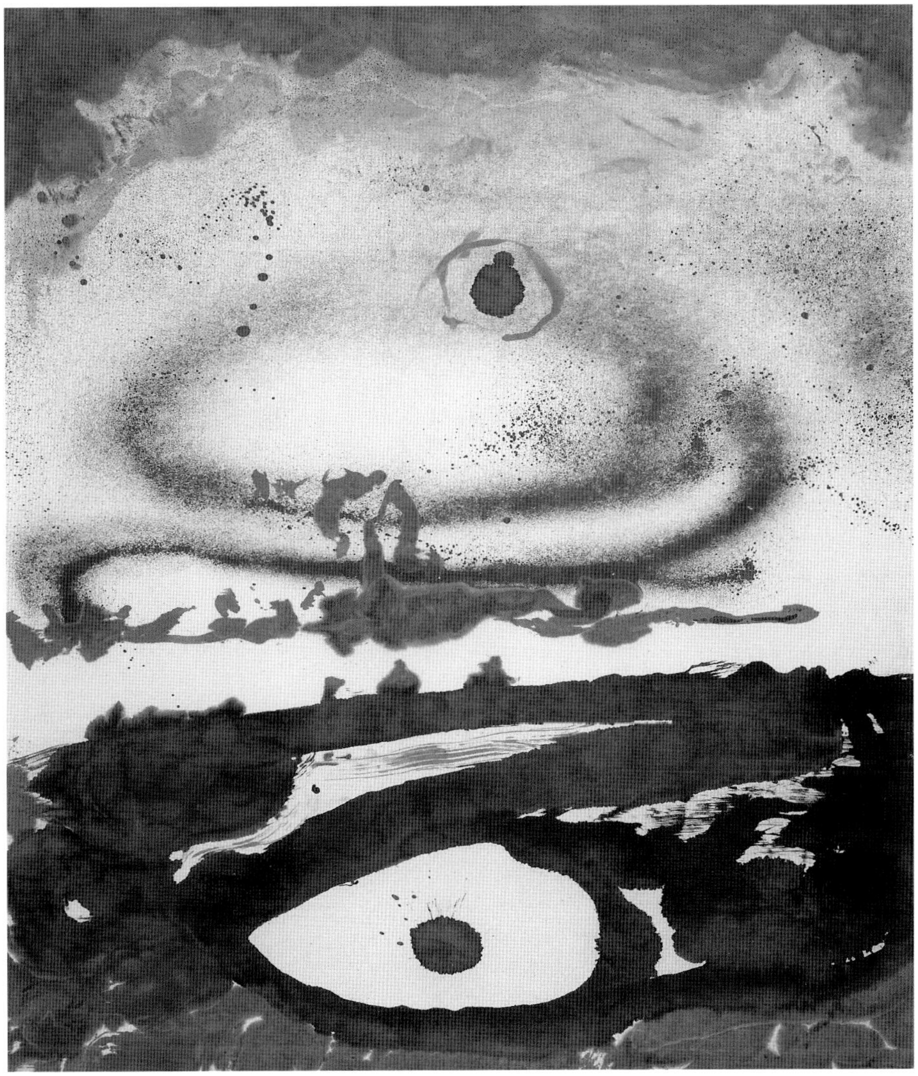

The Improvisation, 1983, 31.80 x 26.60 in

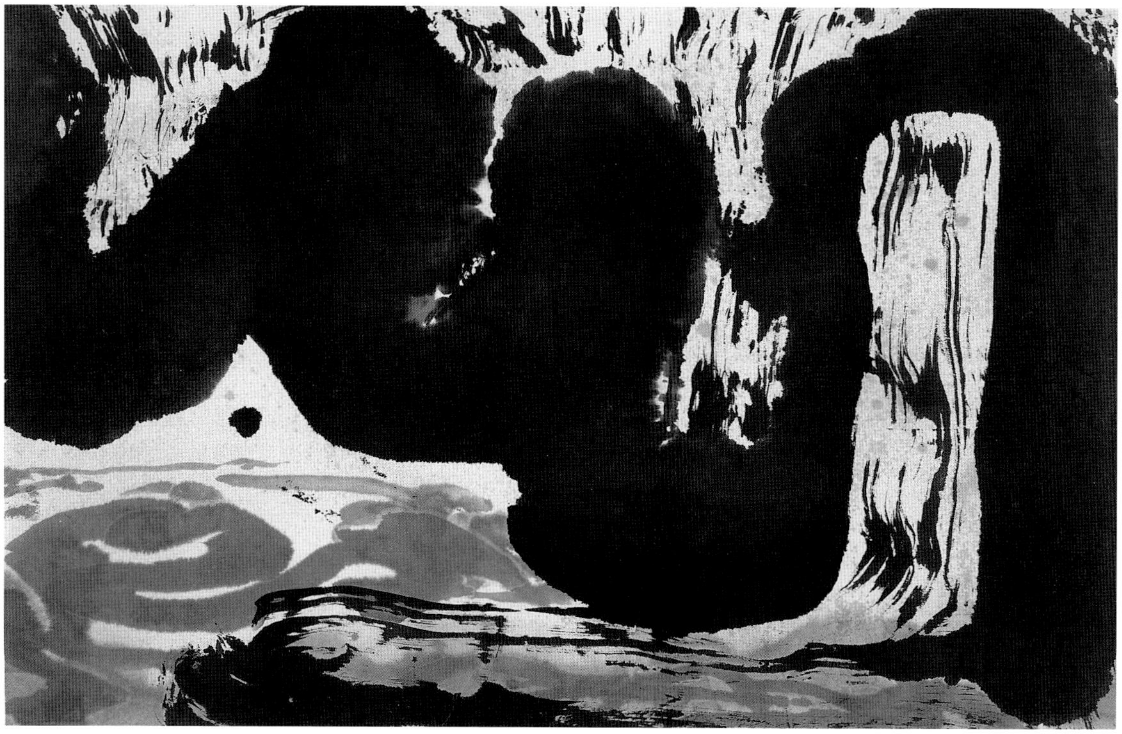

 Woodcut Effect, 1983, 17.60 x 25.20 in

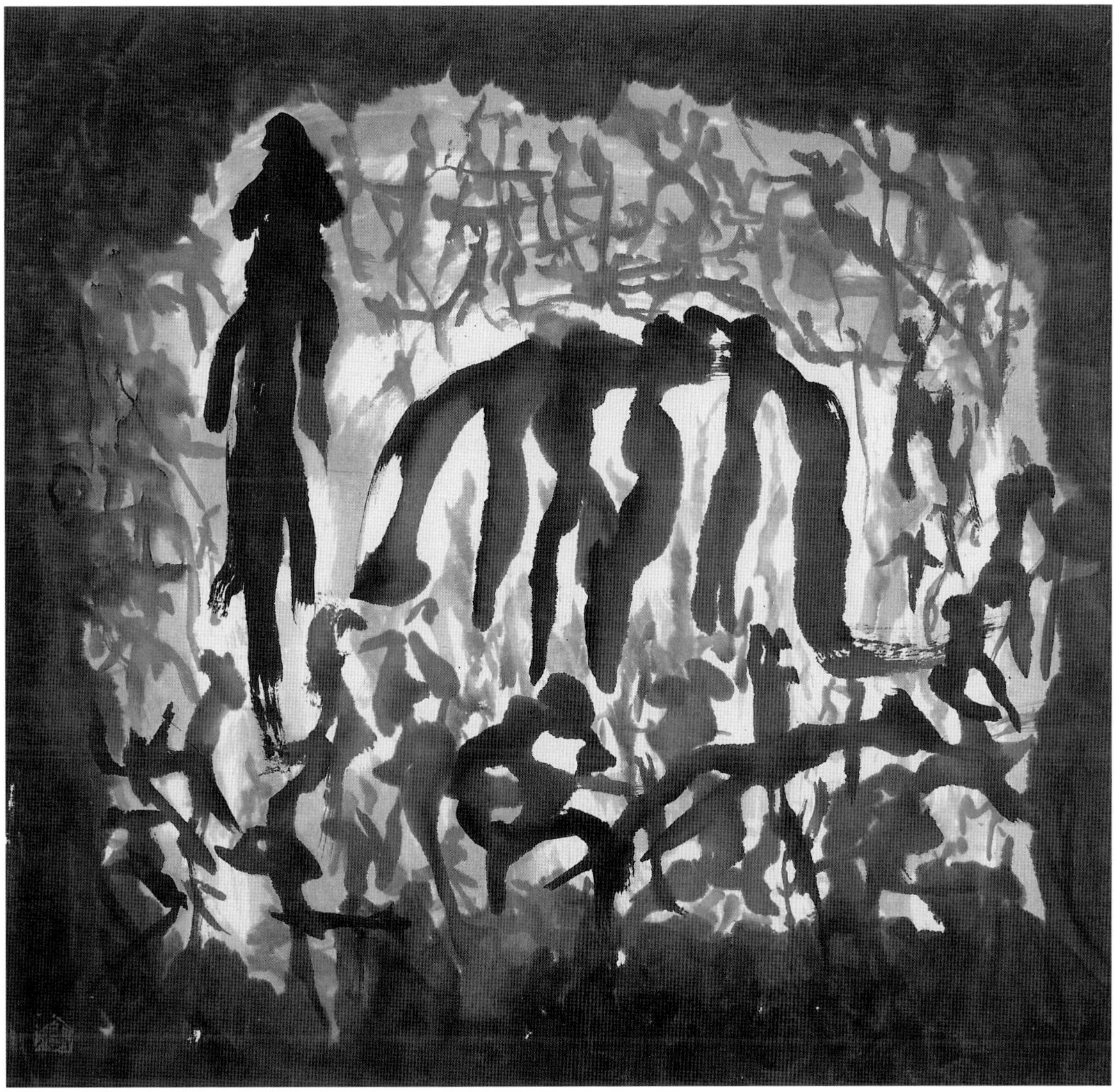

Sacrifice I, 1983, 26.10 x 25.20 in

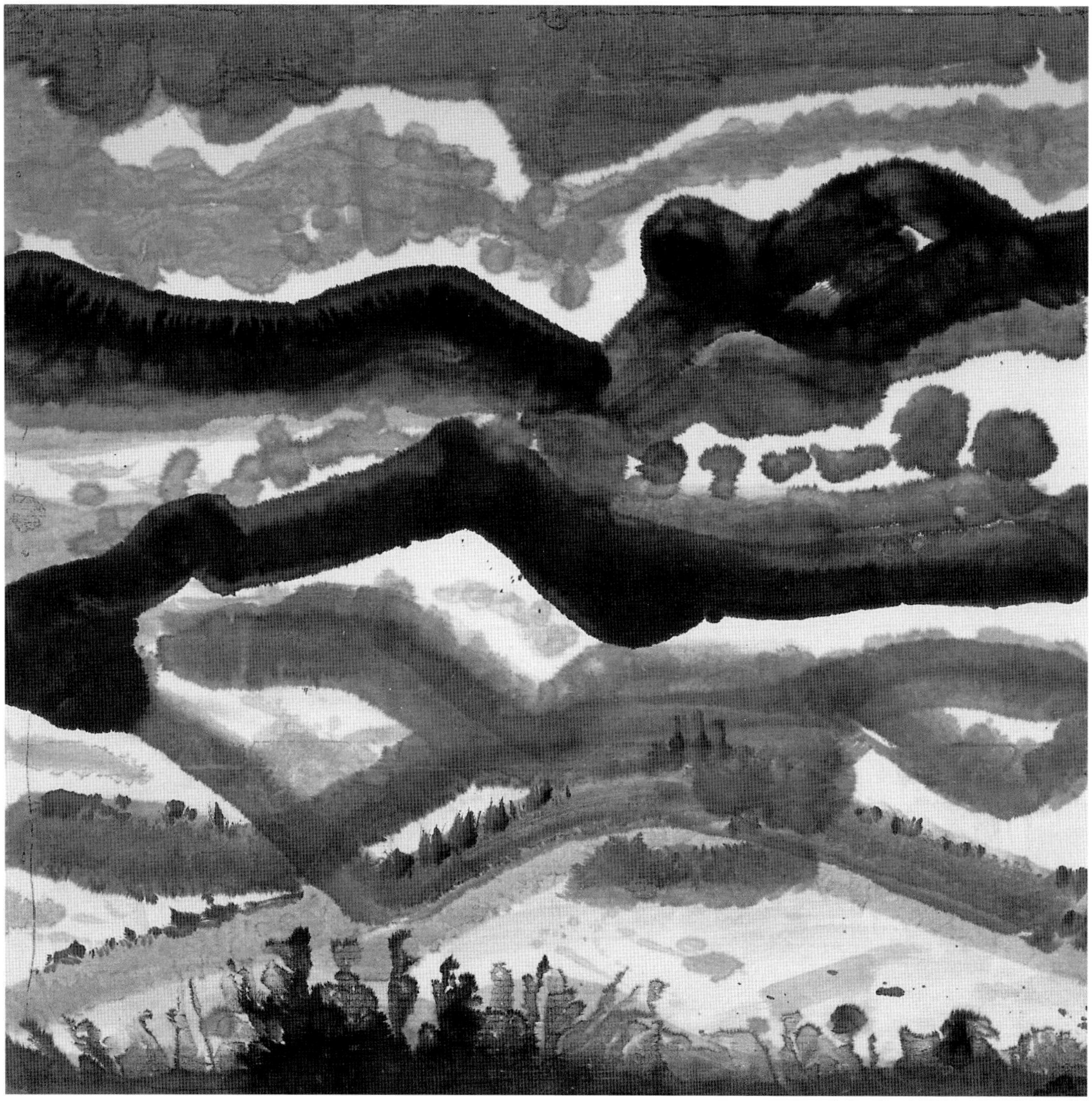

The Magic Mountain, 1983, 40.20 x 40.55 in

Untitled, 1985, 19.60 x 32.20 in

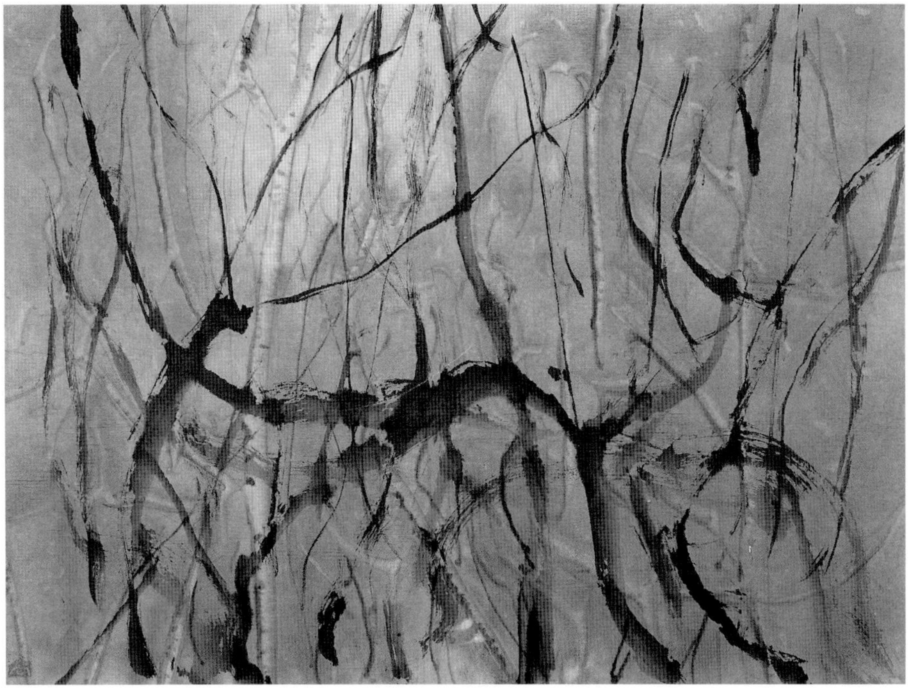

Emotion, 1985, 26.65 x 34.90 in

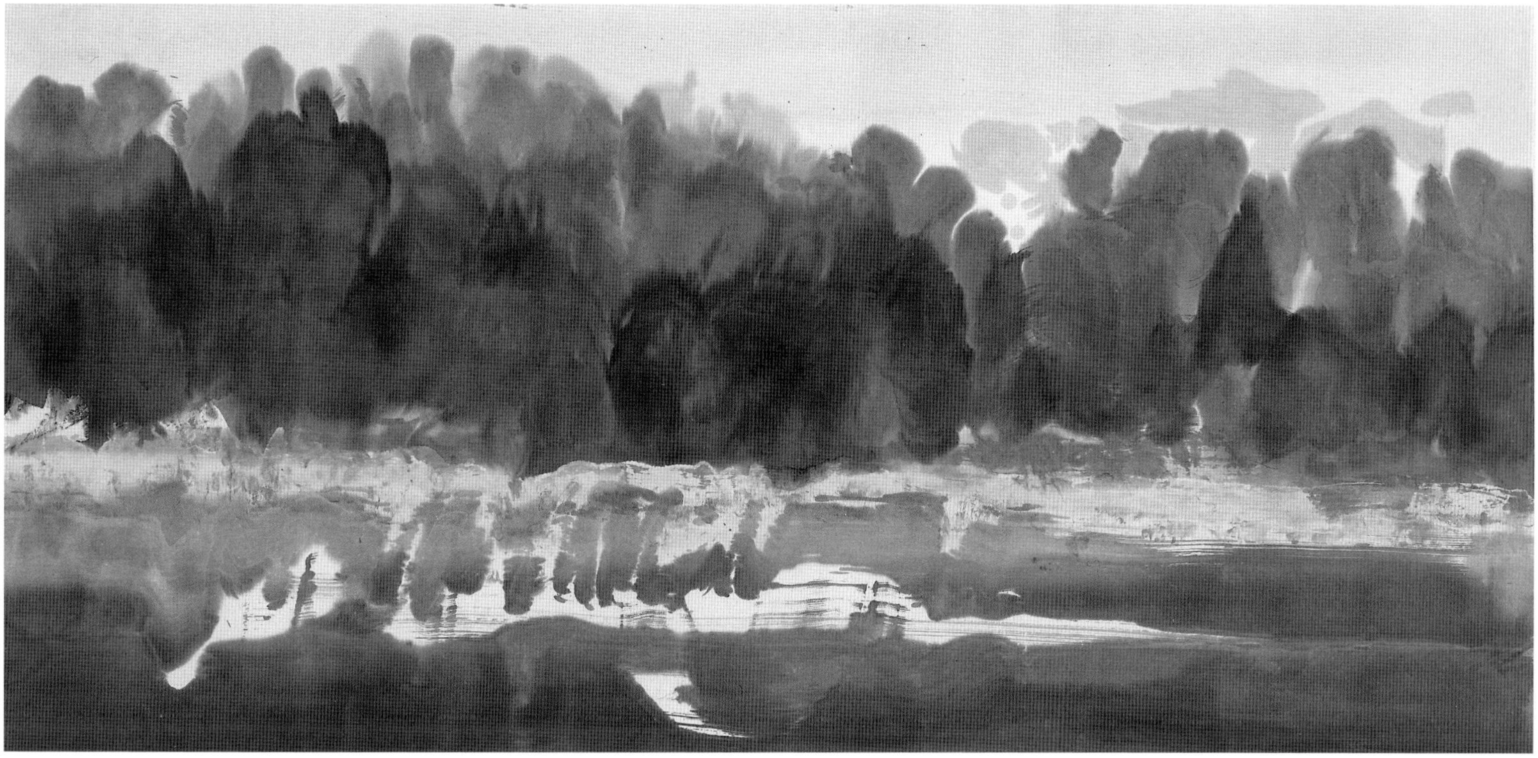

Forest of Rocks, 1985, 27 x 53.70 in

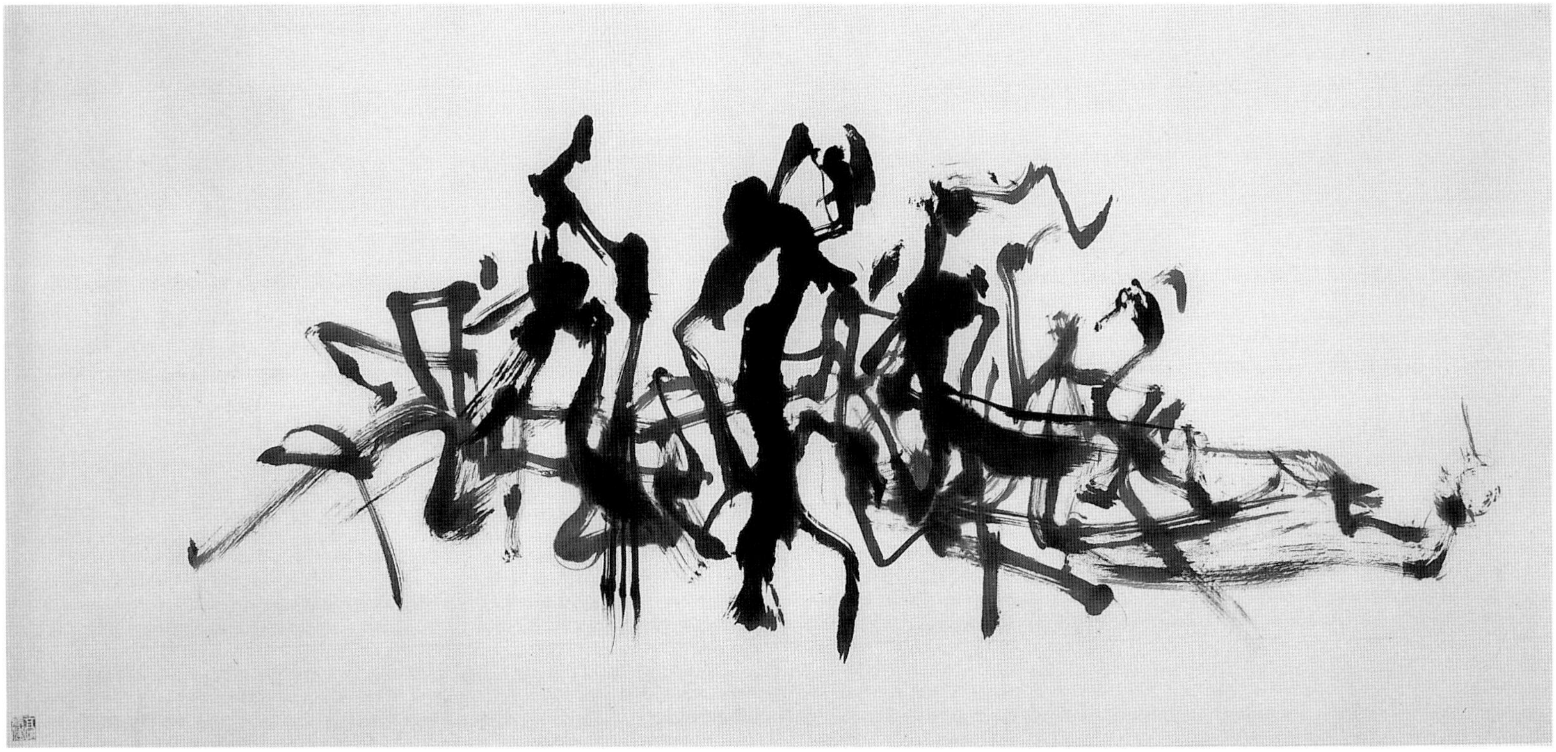

 Italic Writing, 1985, 26.90 x 53.60 in

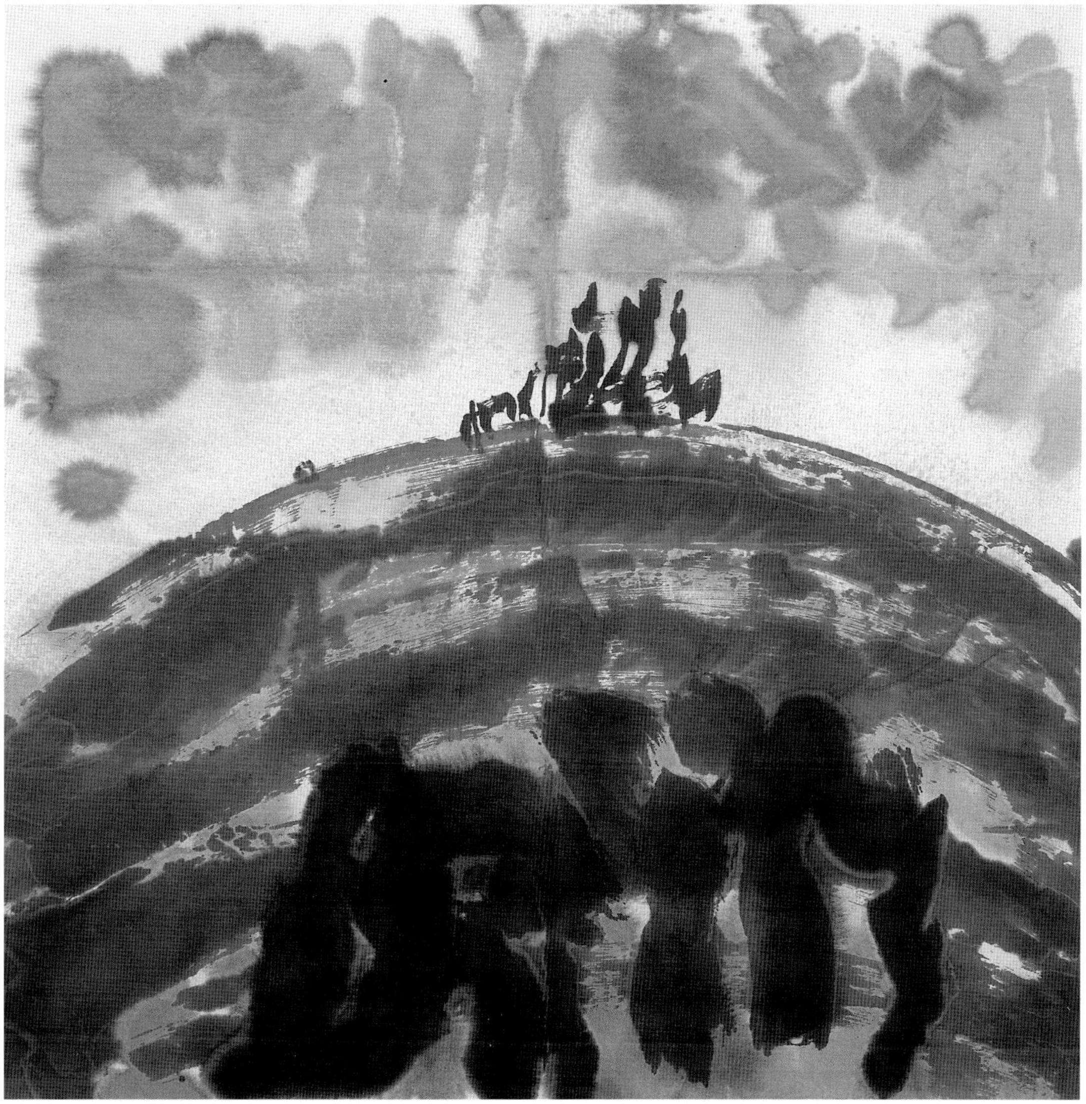

A Black Game, 1985, 41.10 x 40 in

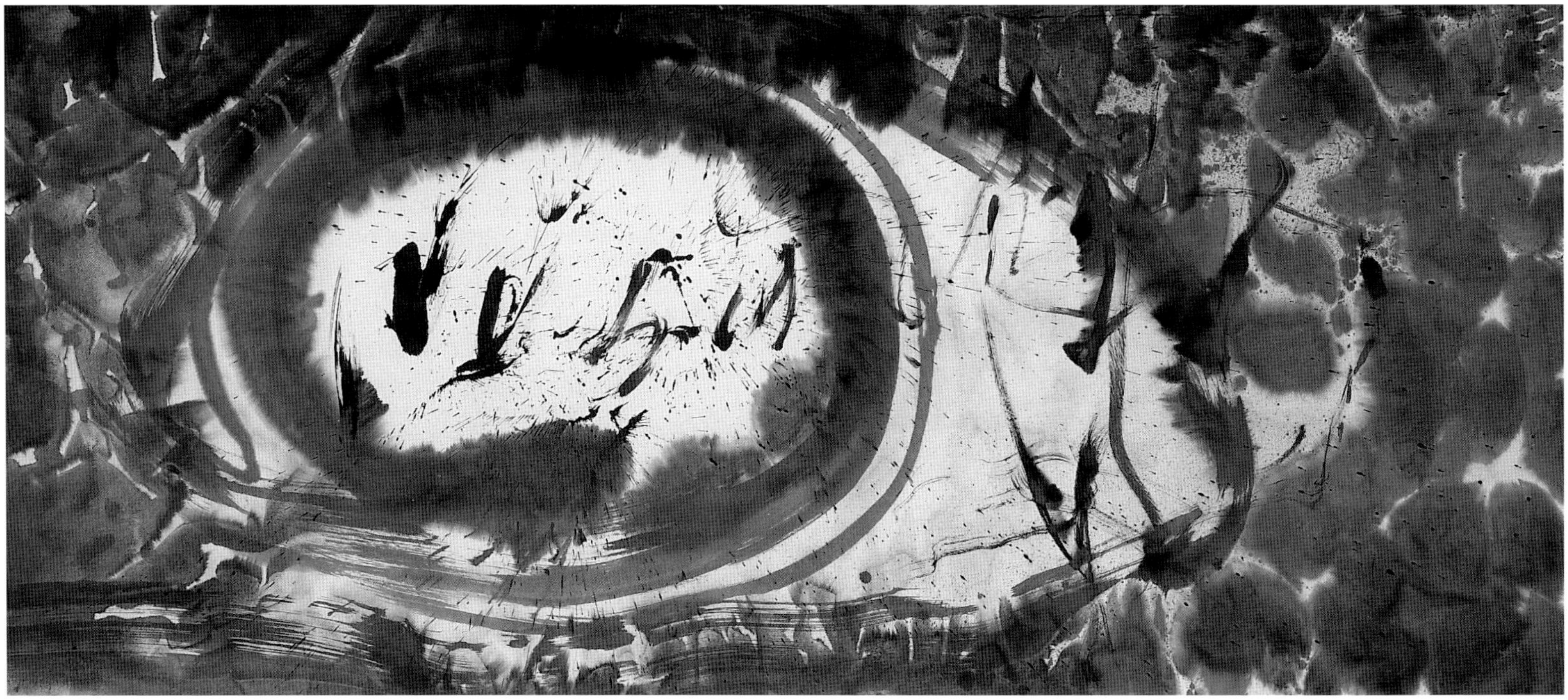

 The Creation of the World, 1985, 38.35 x 83.10 in

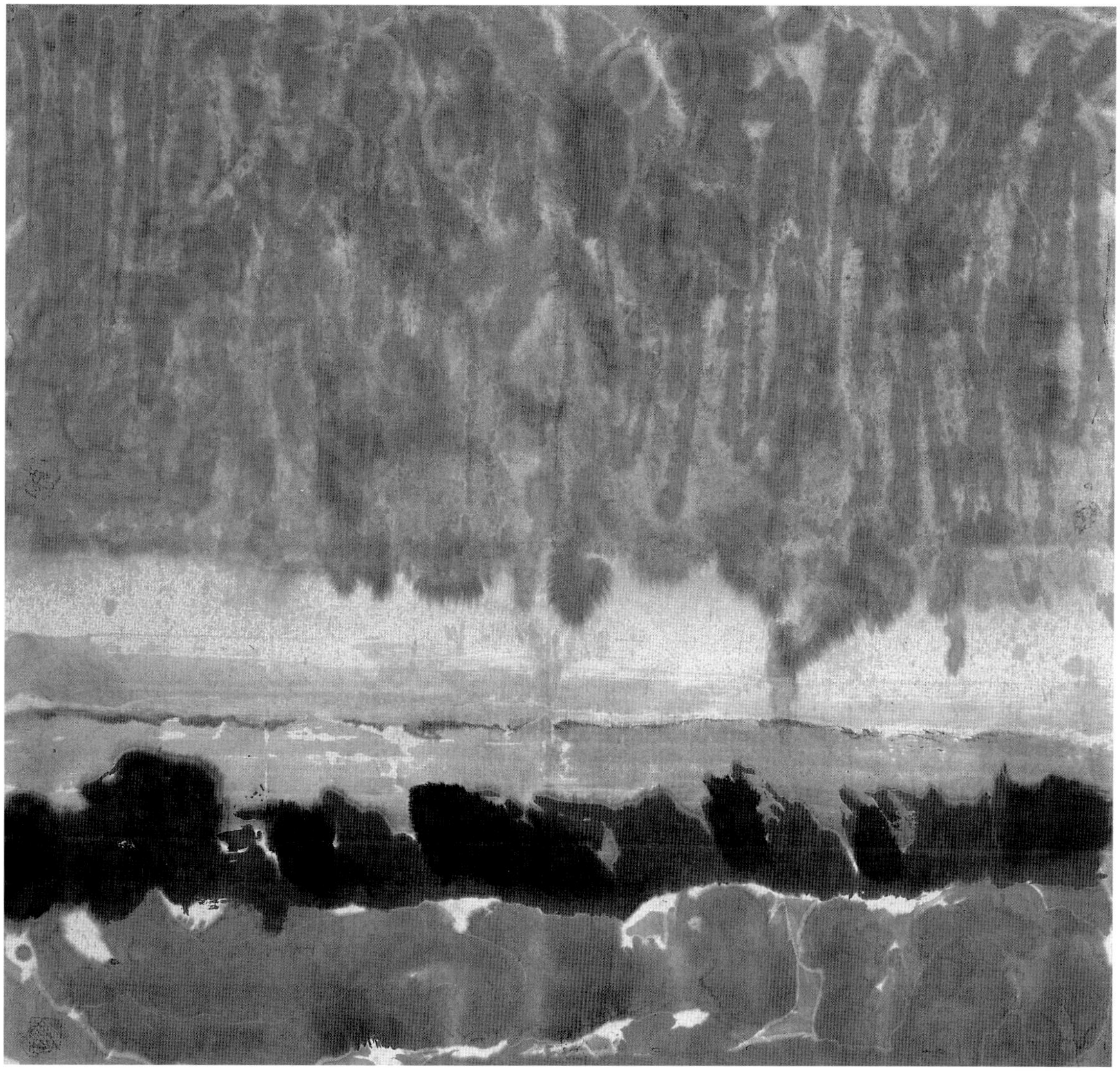

The Taste of Inc II, 1985, 39.80 x 40.55 in

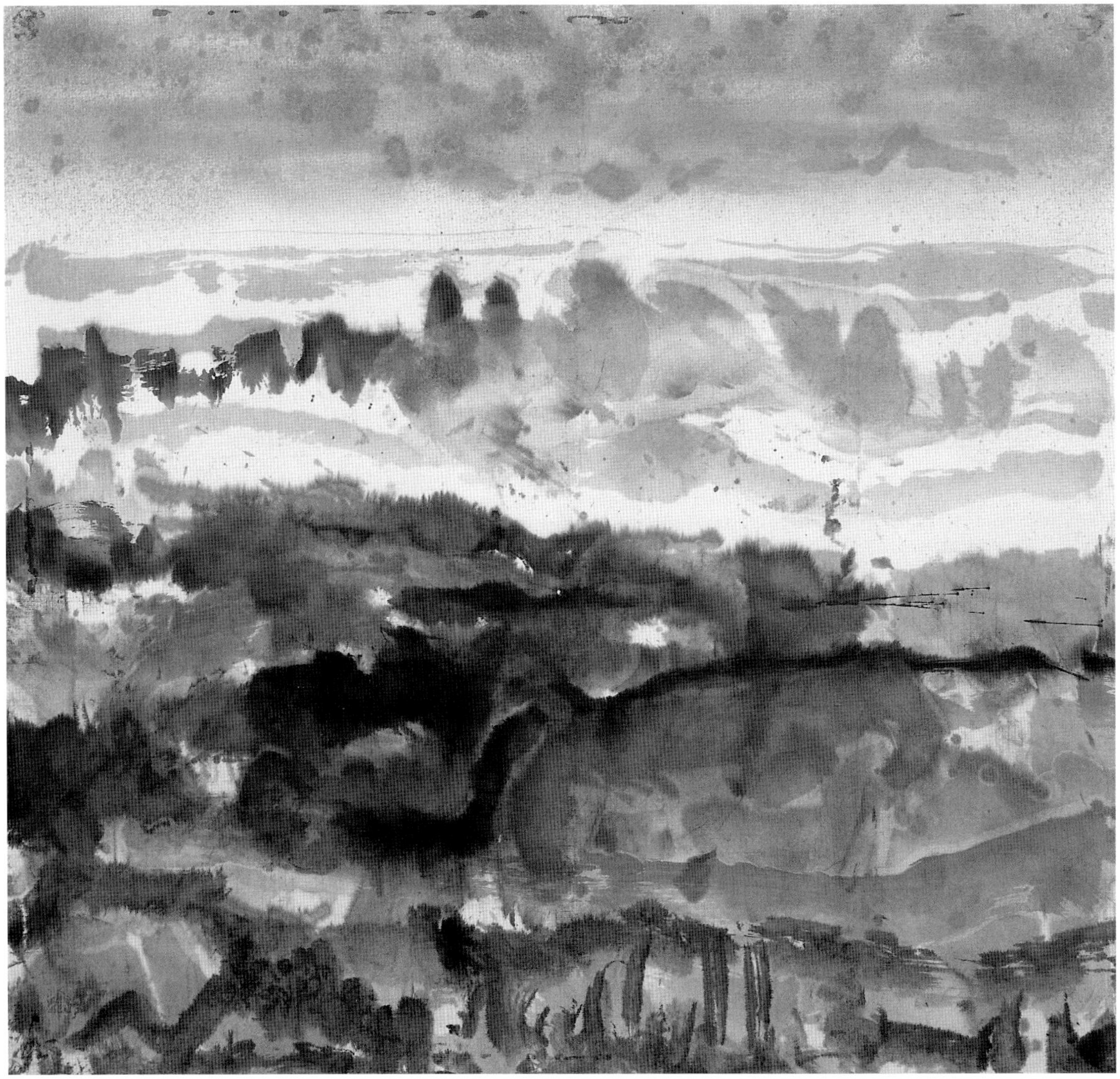

The Taste of Inc IV, 1985, 39.80 x 40.55 in

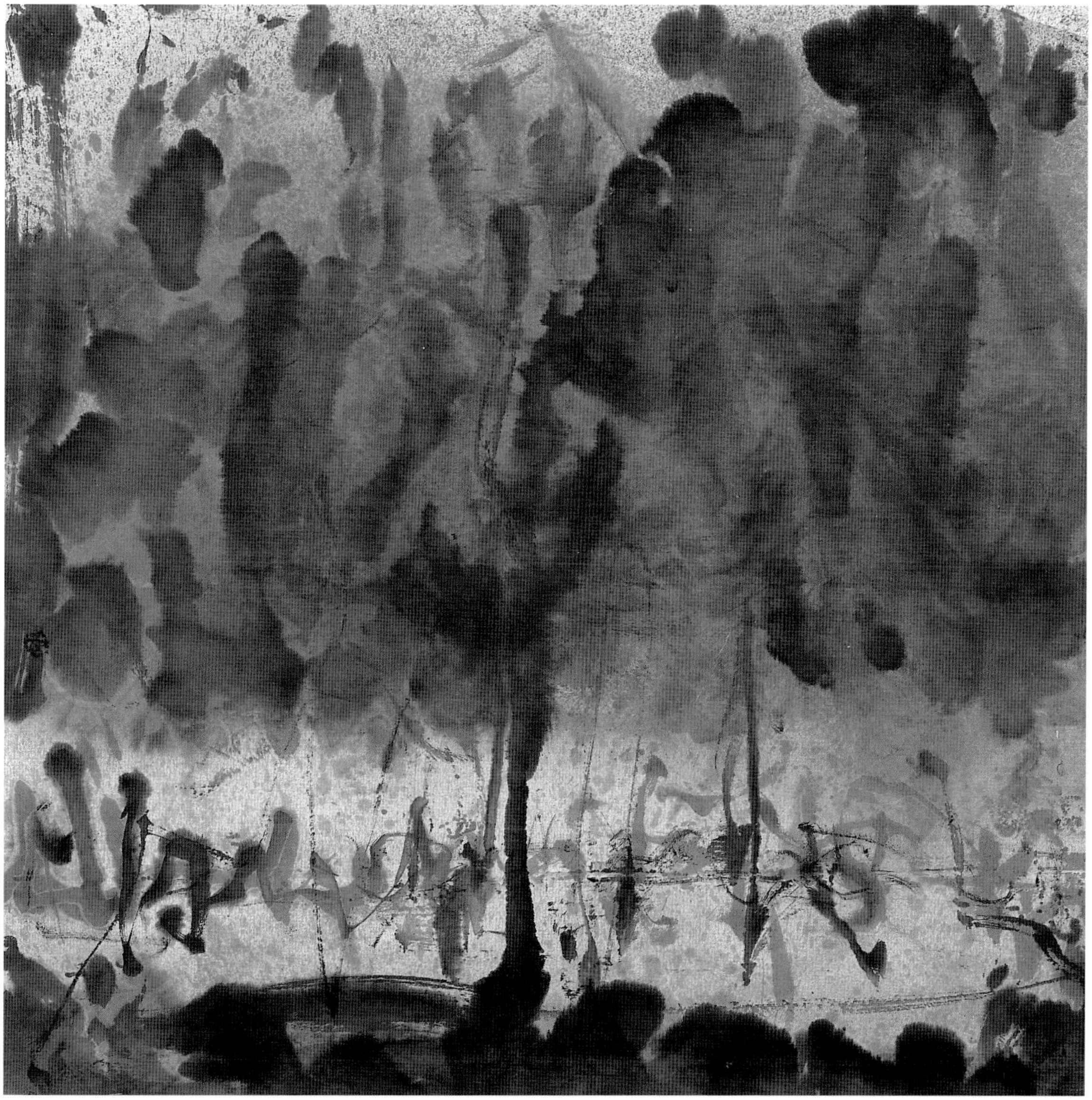

The Taste of Inc V, 1985, 40.95 x 40.55 in

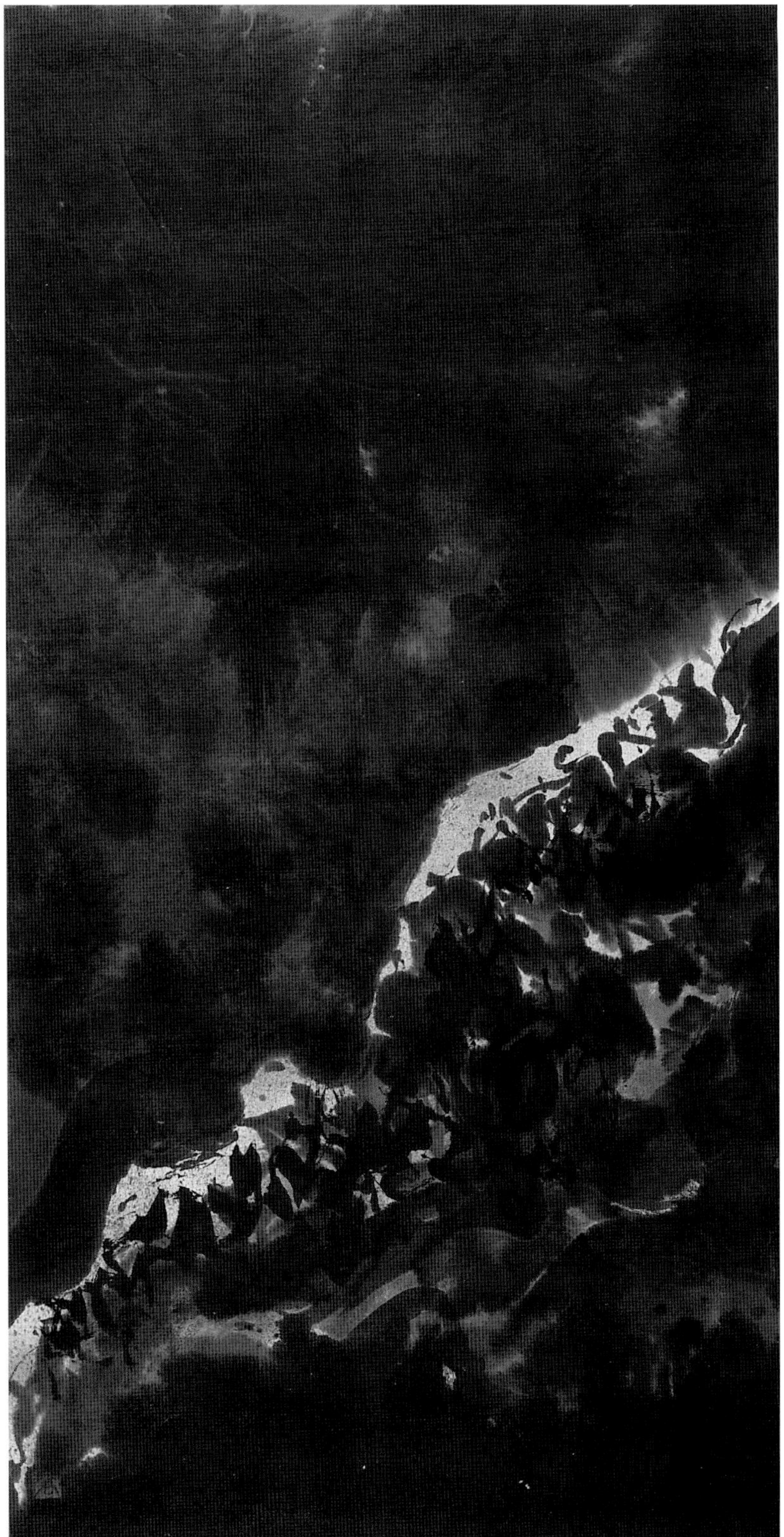

This Bank, 1985, 53.50 x 26.80 in

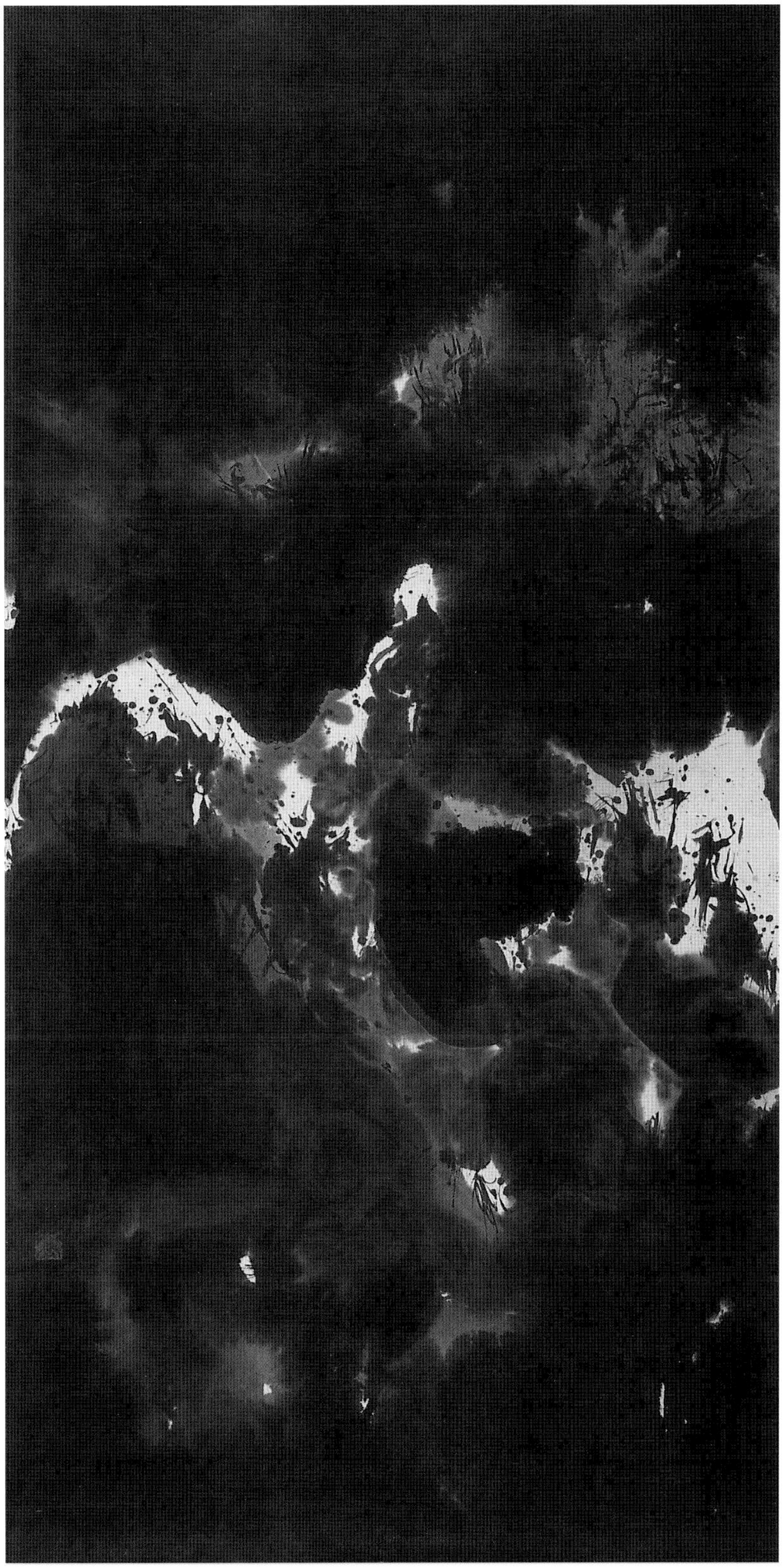

The Other Bank, 1985, 53.50 x 26.80 in

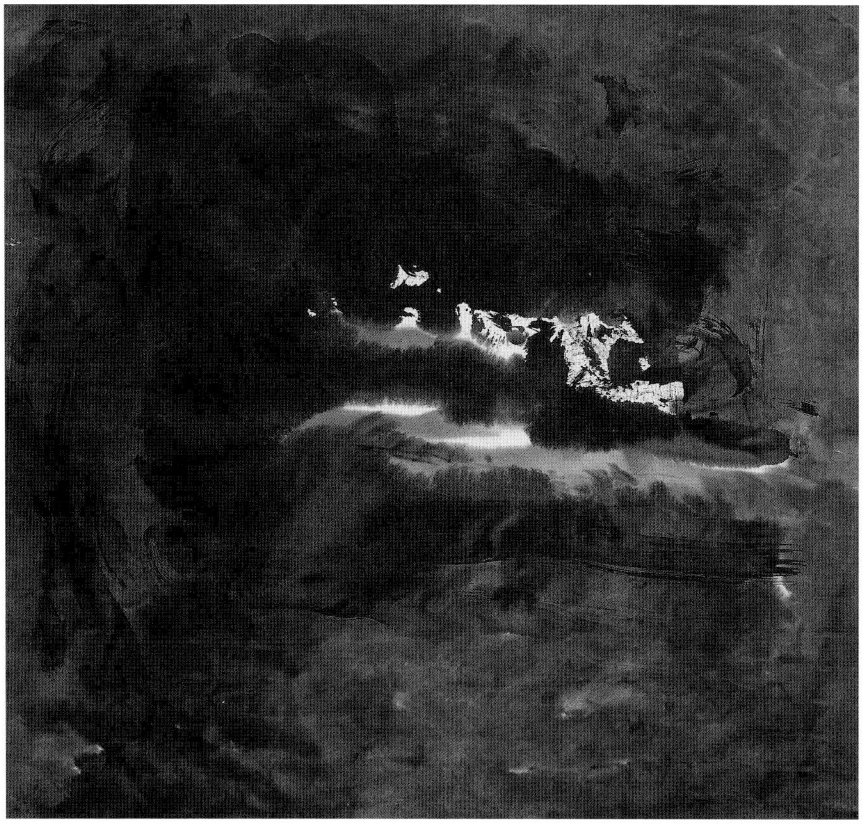

 Untitled, 1985, 26.40 x 26.40 in

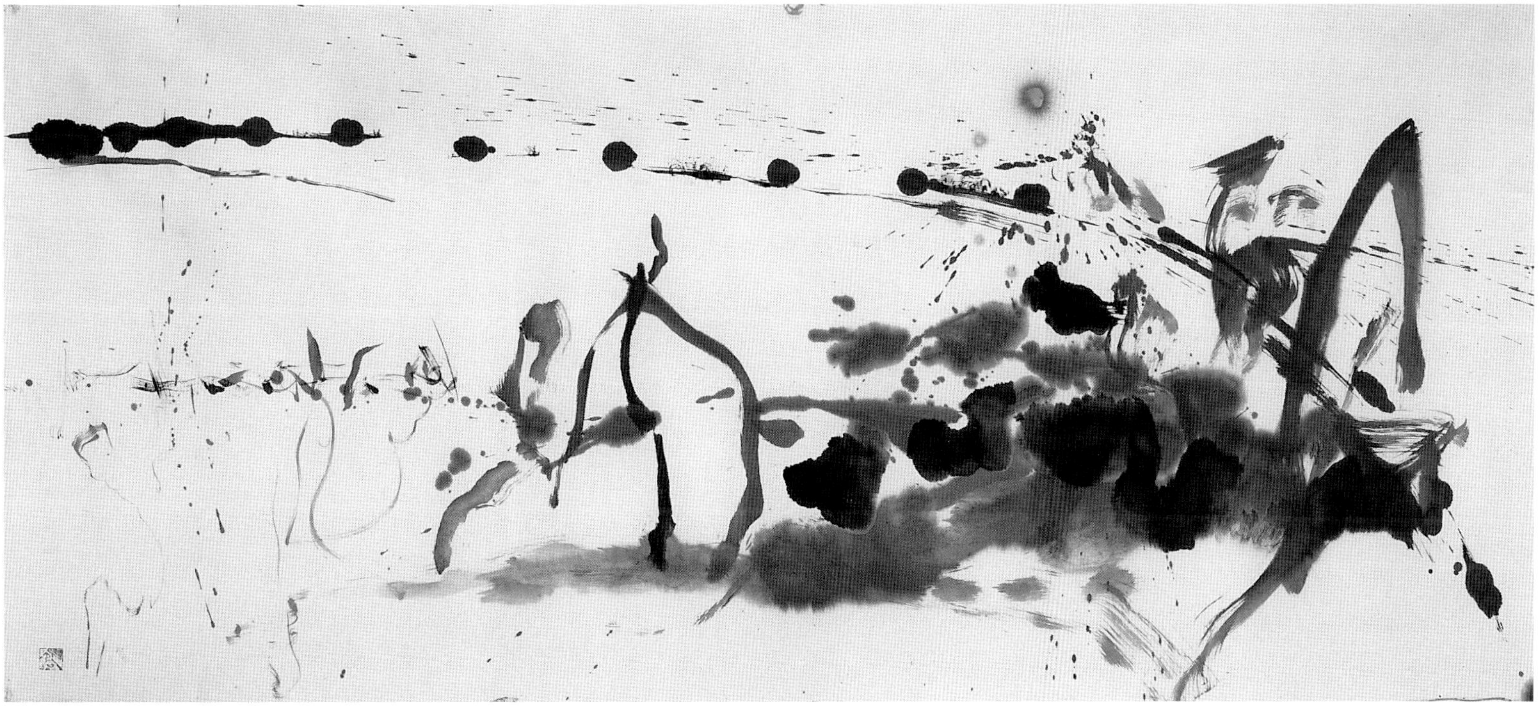

Birth, 1985, 37.80 x 80.70 in

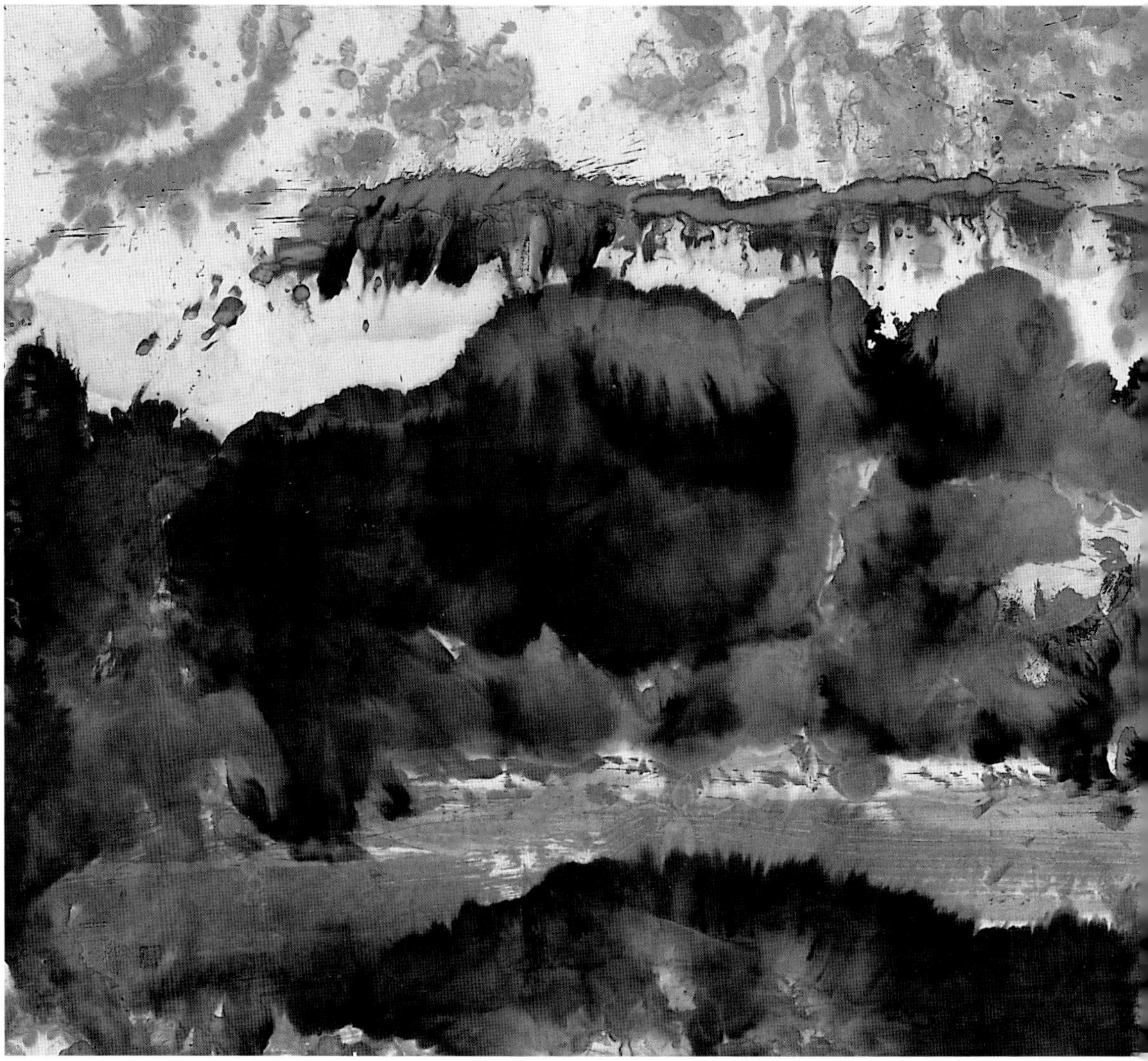

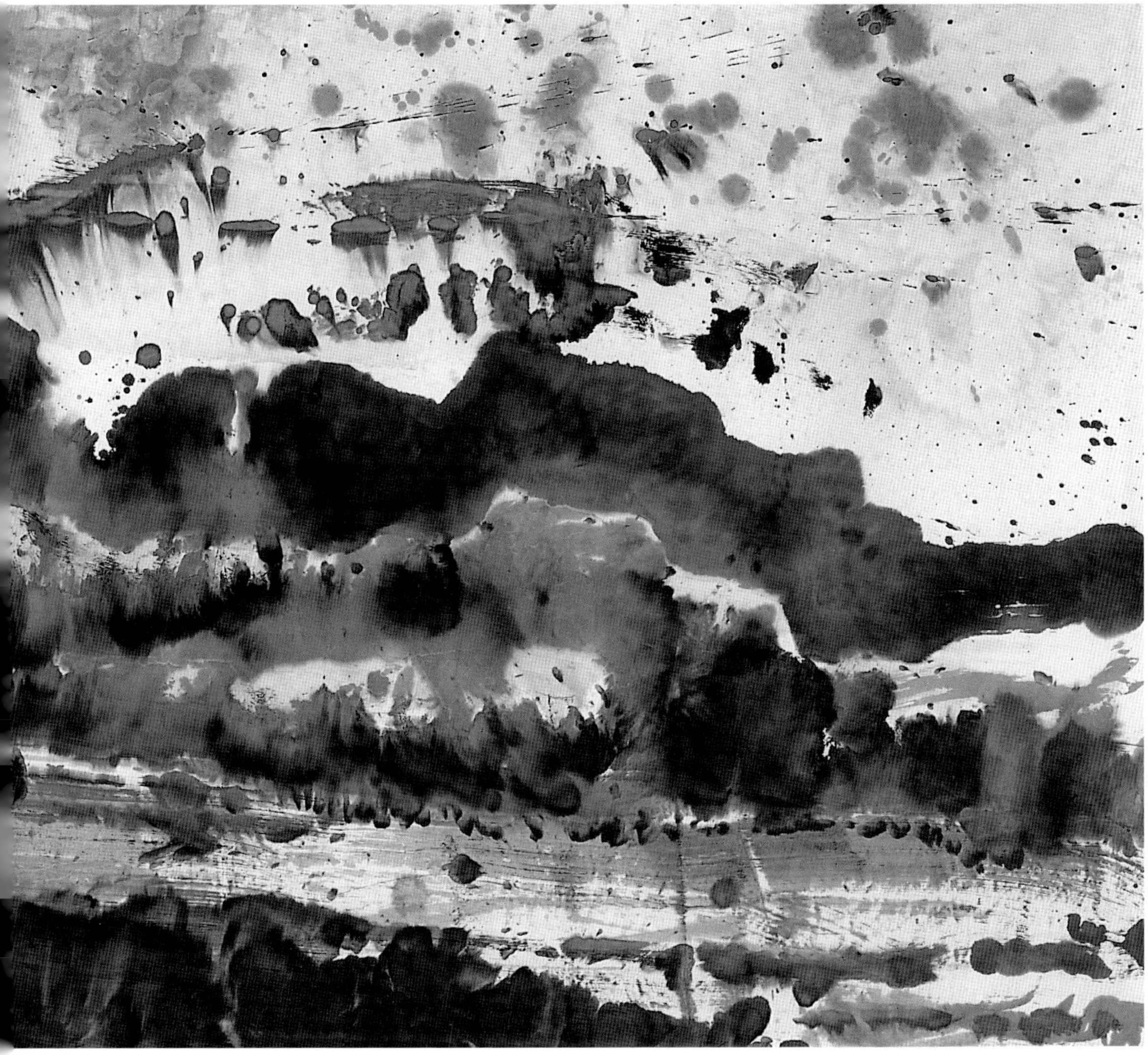

Taste of Inc, 1986, 41.10 x 90.20 in

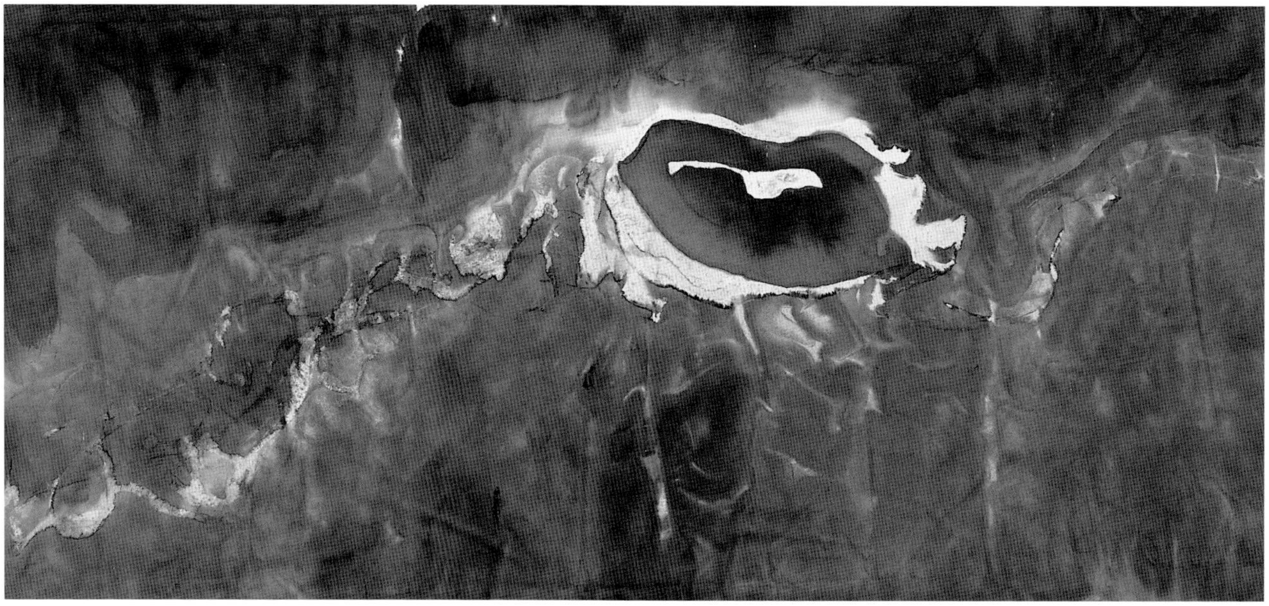

 The Desire, 1986, 26.40 x 53.60 in

Untitled, 1986, 41.10 x 69.70 in

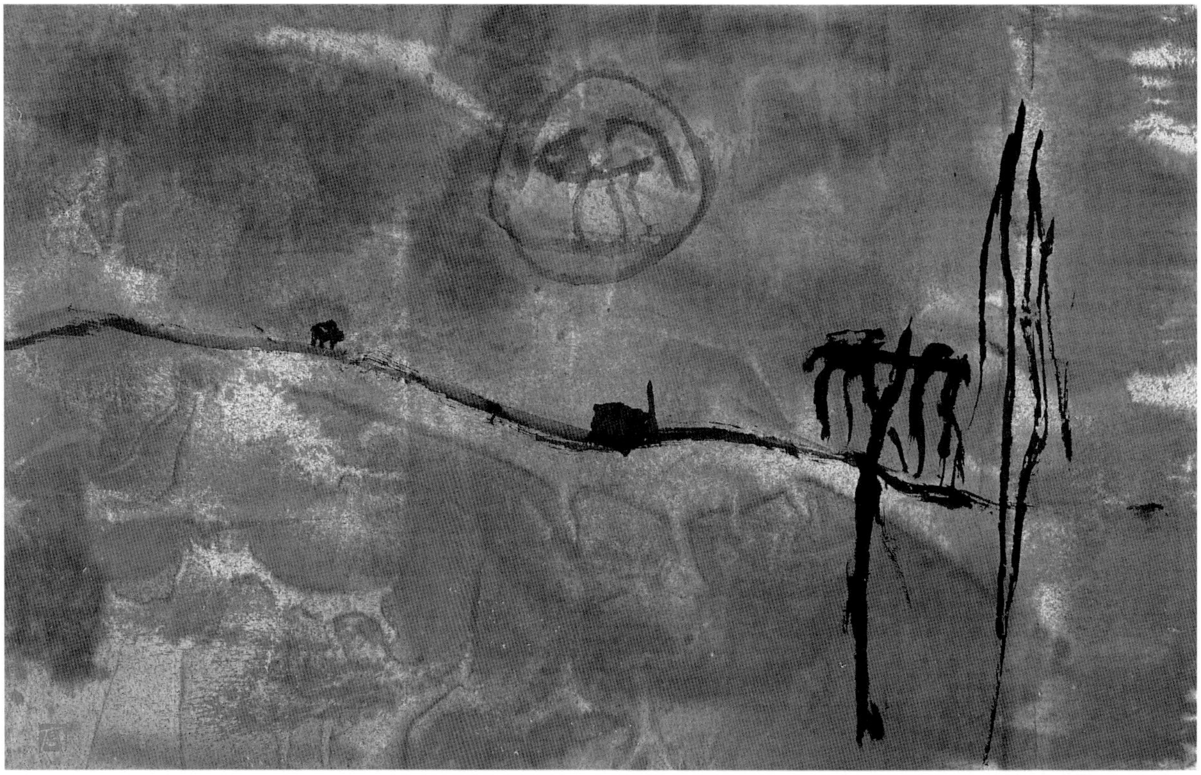

Prehistoric Legend, 1986, 26 x 39.70 in

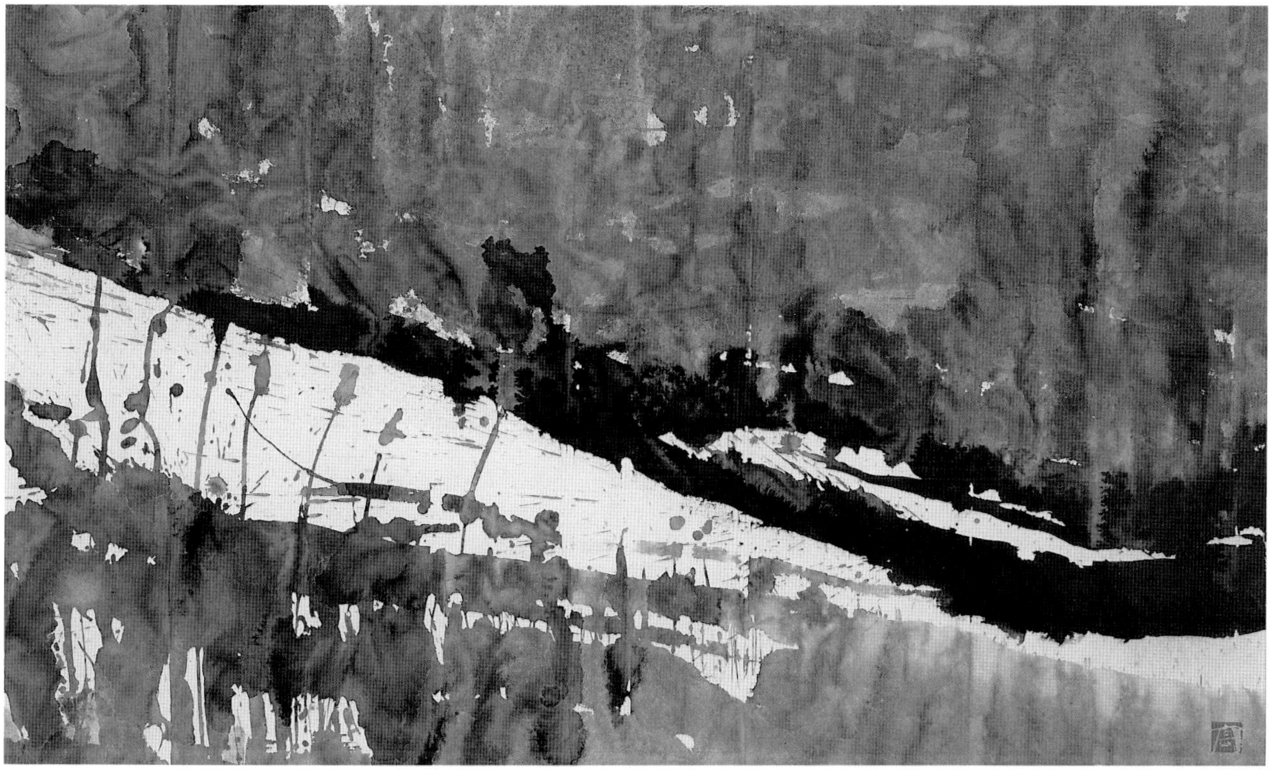

River in the Dark, 1986, 22.90 x 37.10 in

The Moon, 1986, 26.80 x 26.60 in

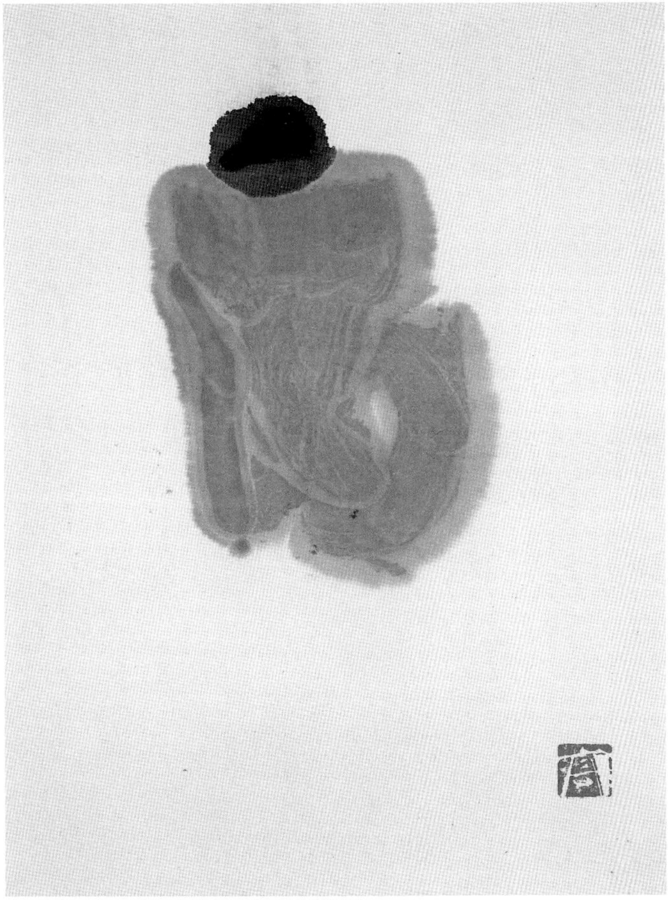

A Sitting Man, 1986, 15.55 x 11.70 in

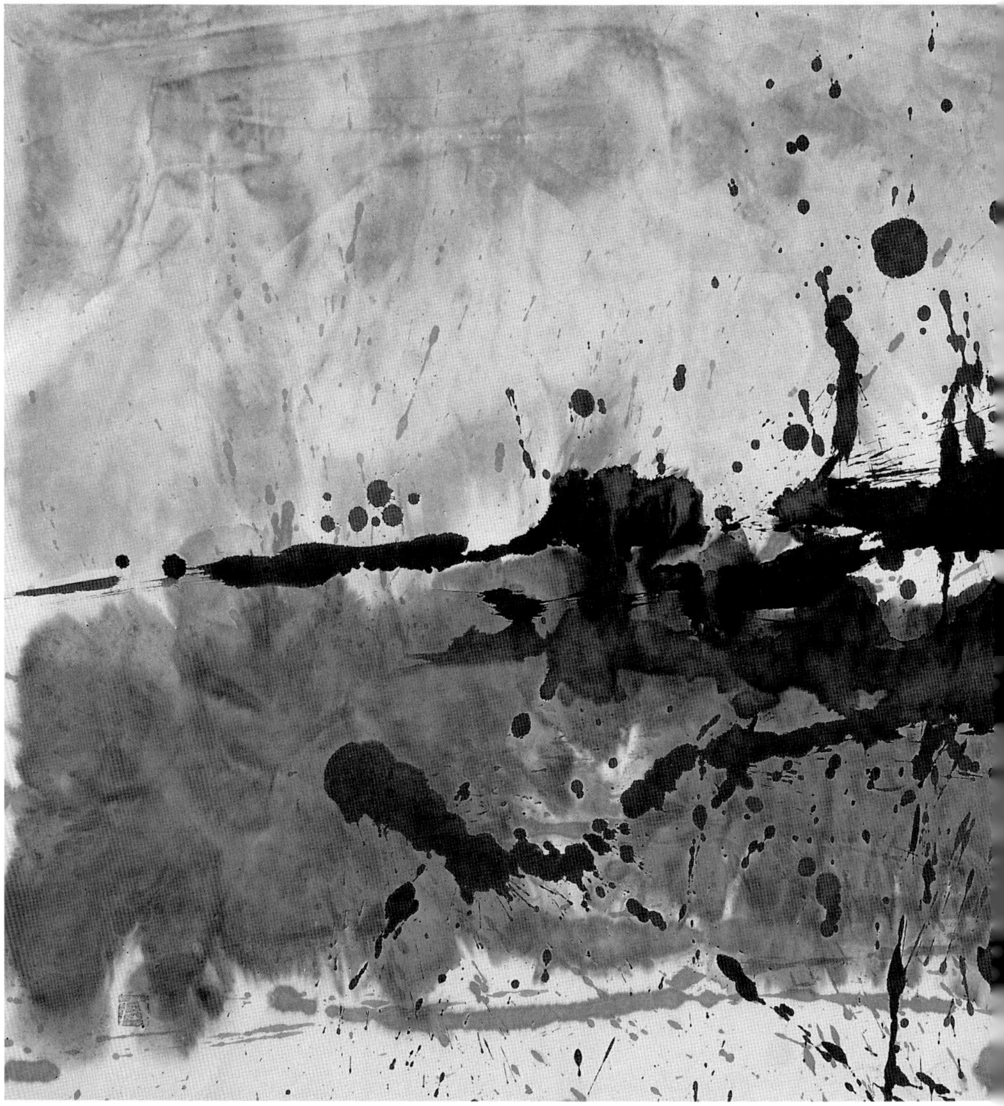

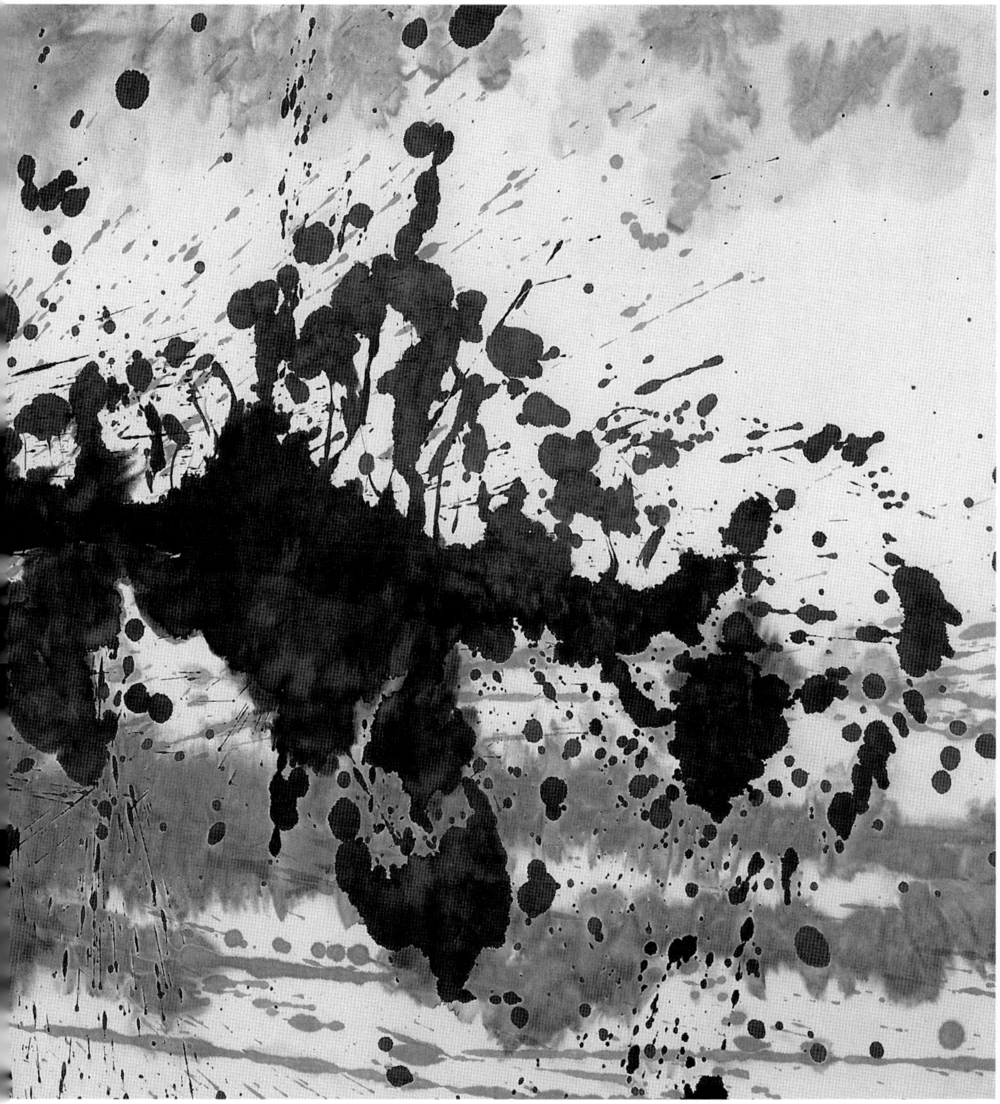

Anxiousness, 1986, 33.10 x 59.65 in

Between Sky and Earth, 1987, 48.80 x 97.05 in

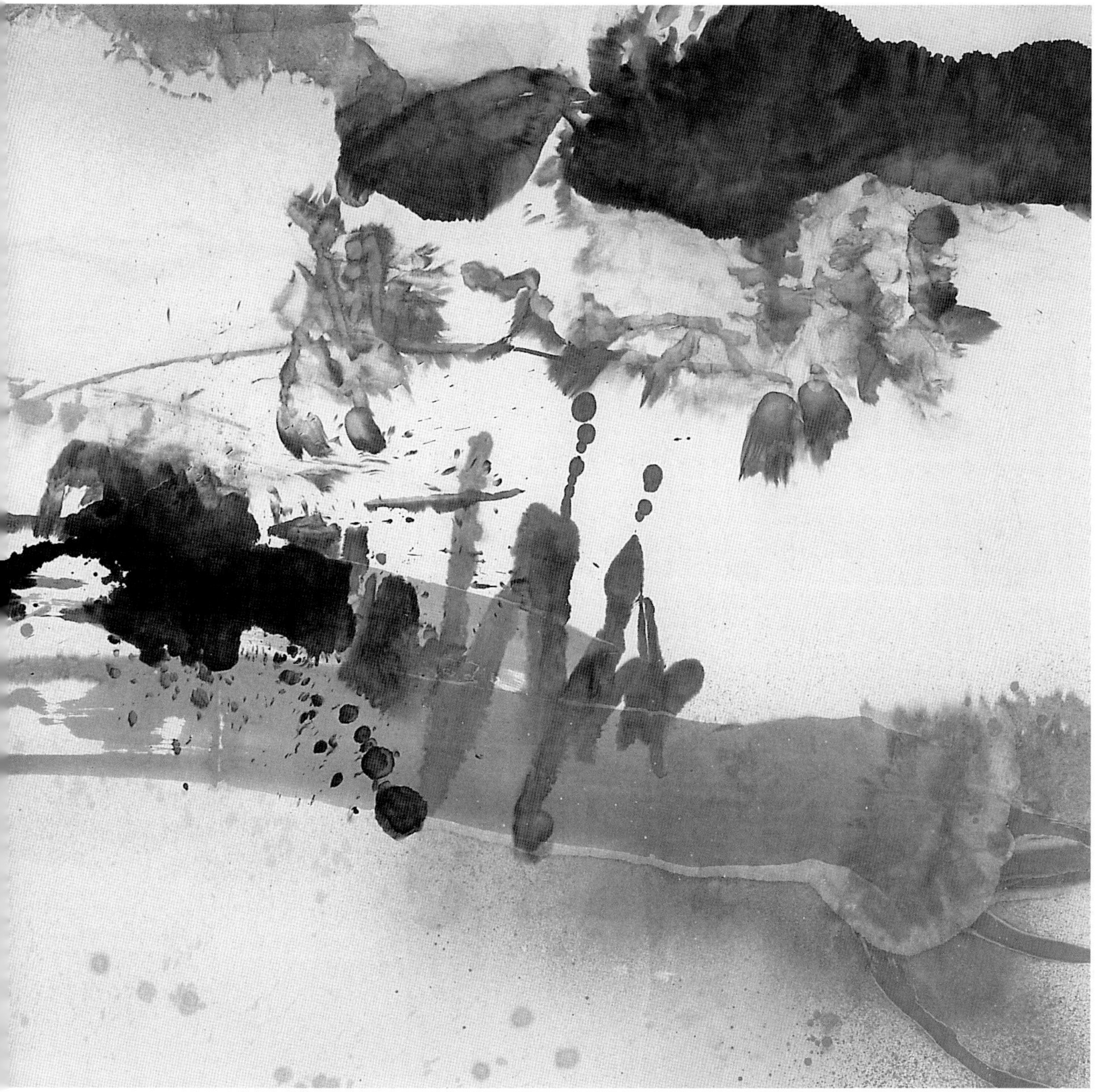

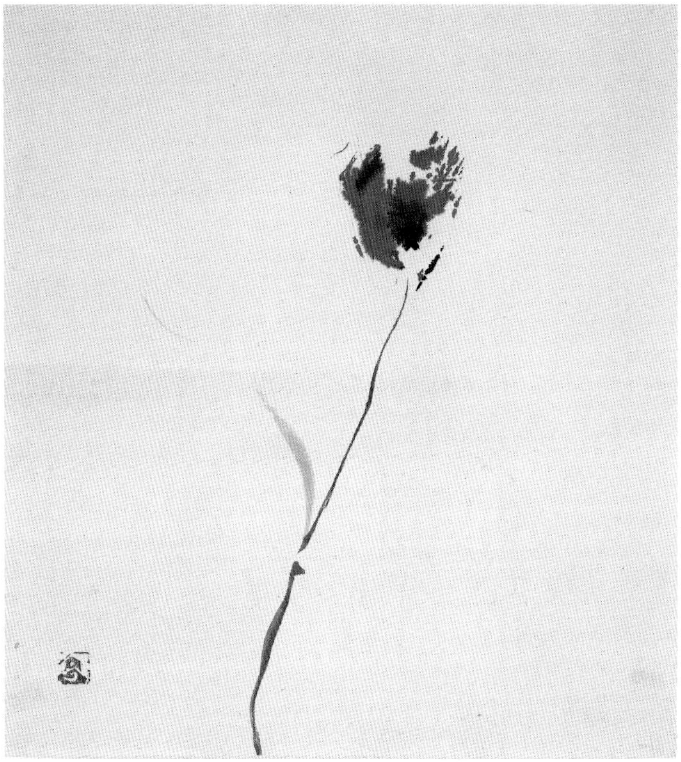

A Flower, 1987, 13.80 x 12.20 in

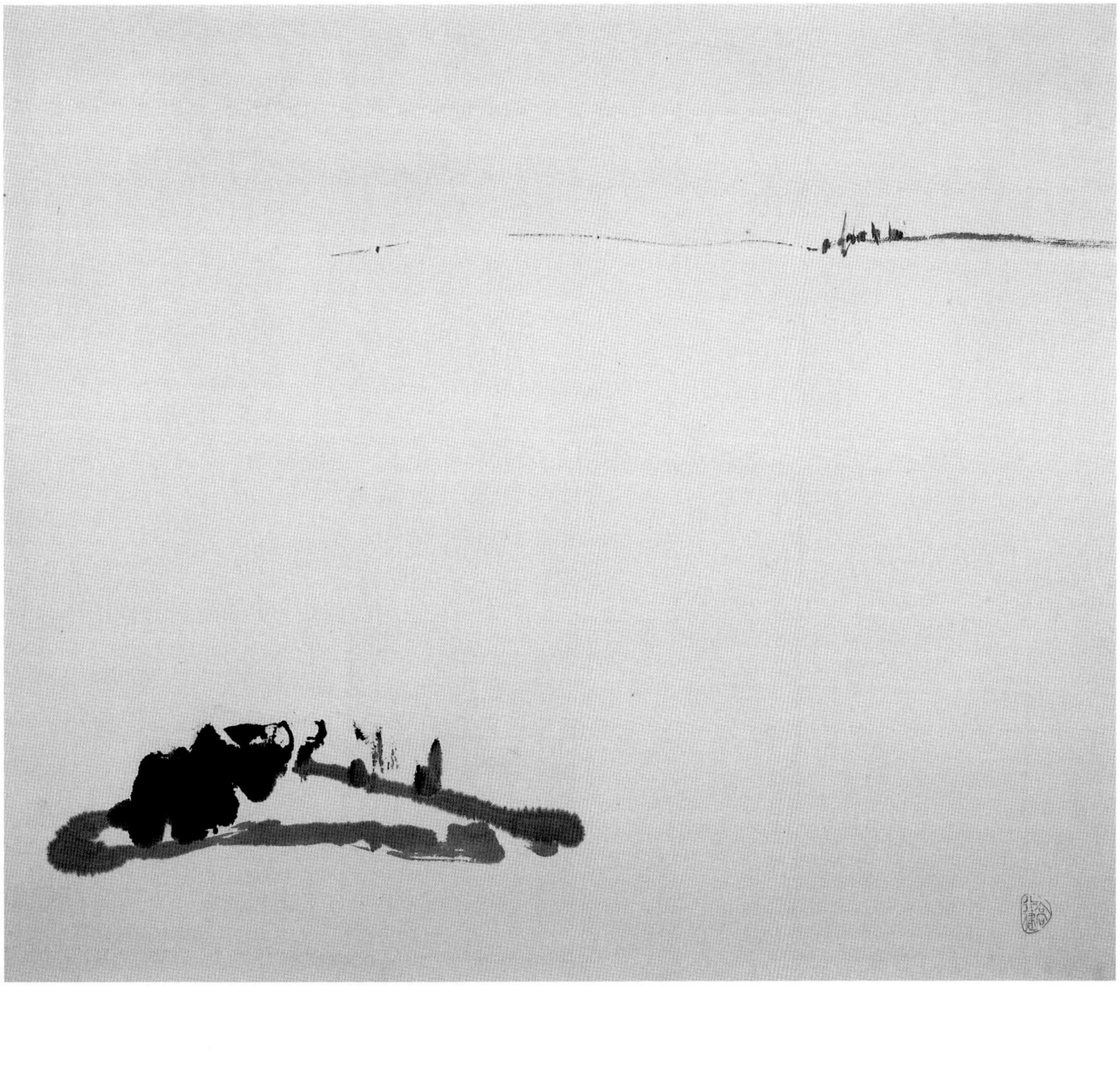

The Horizon, 1987, 35.70 x 39.45 in

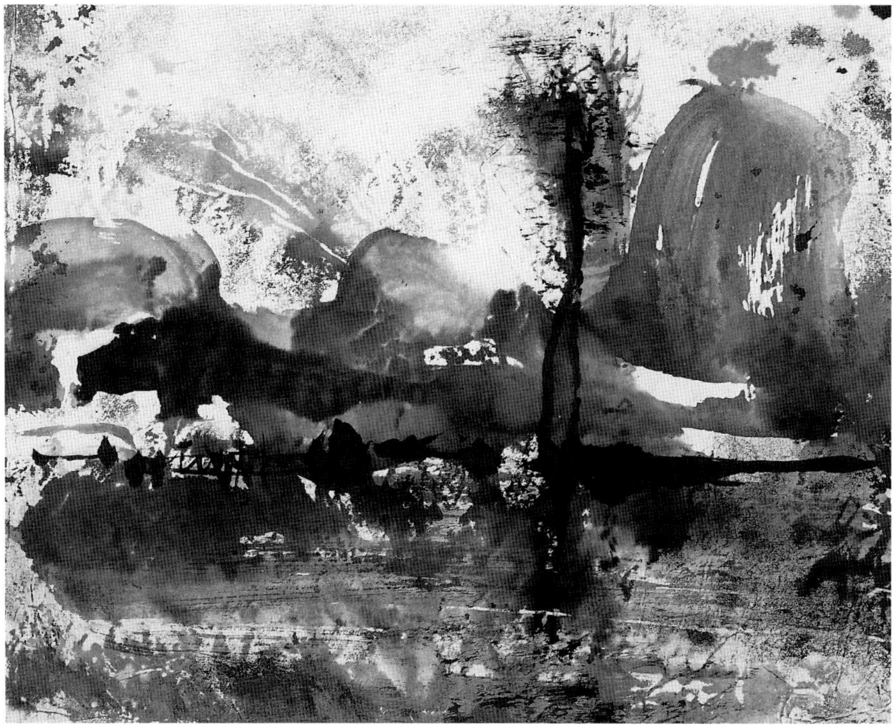

In the Heart of the Mountain, 1987, 12.80 x 15.50 in

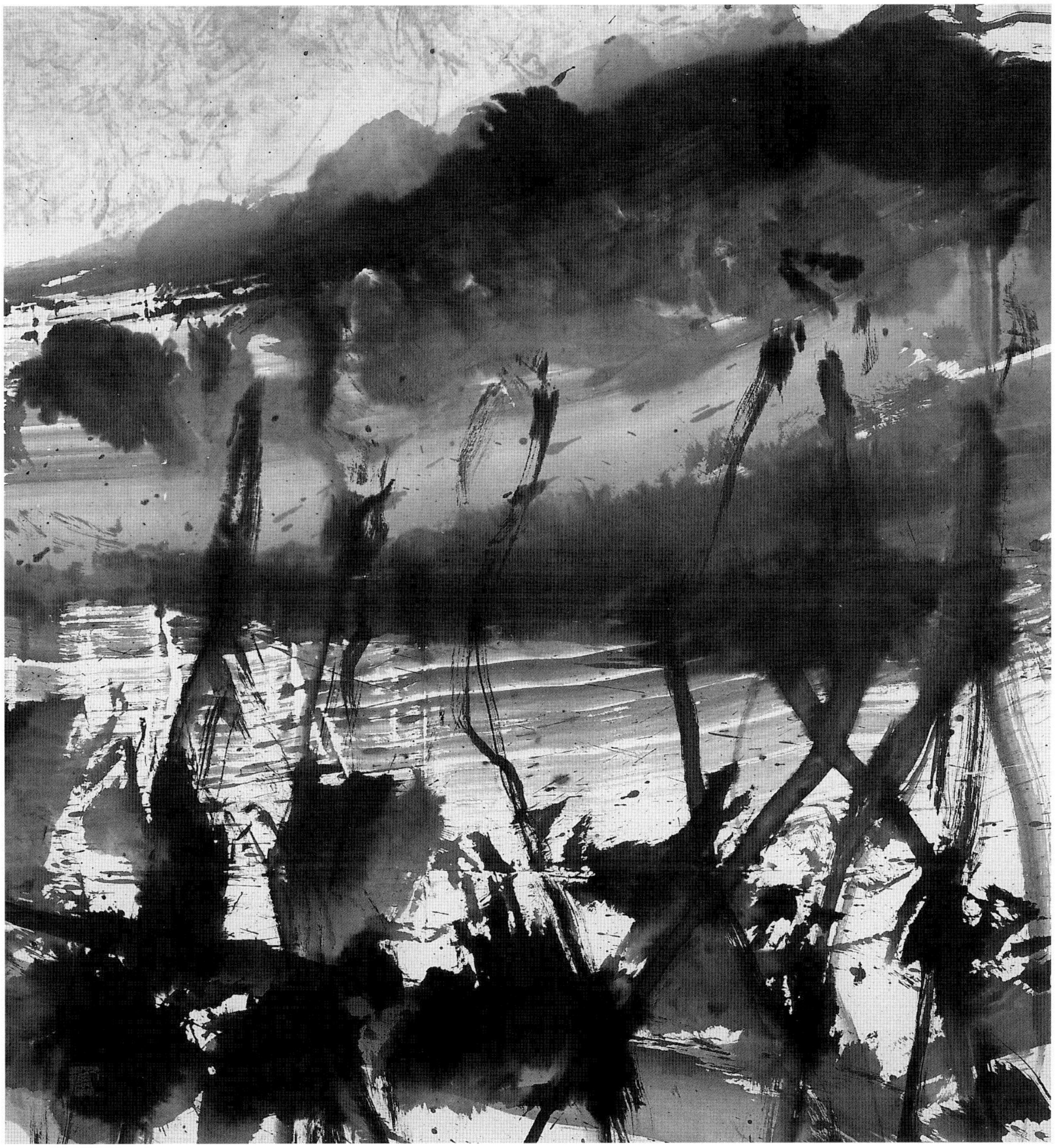

The Dead Season, 1987, 35.90 x 33.30 in

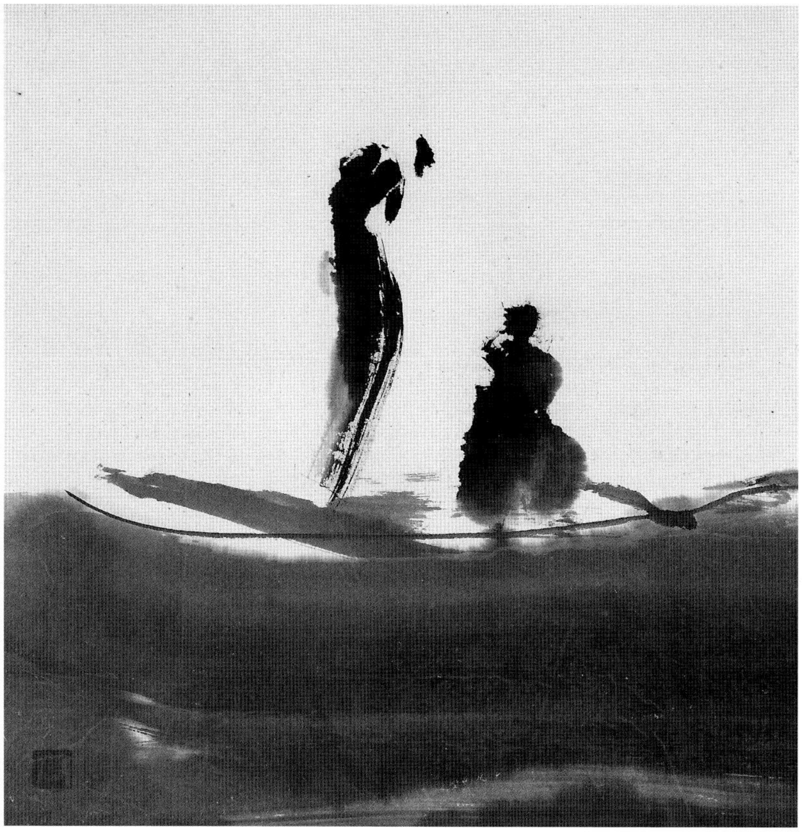

Two Women, 1987, 19.10 x 18.20 in

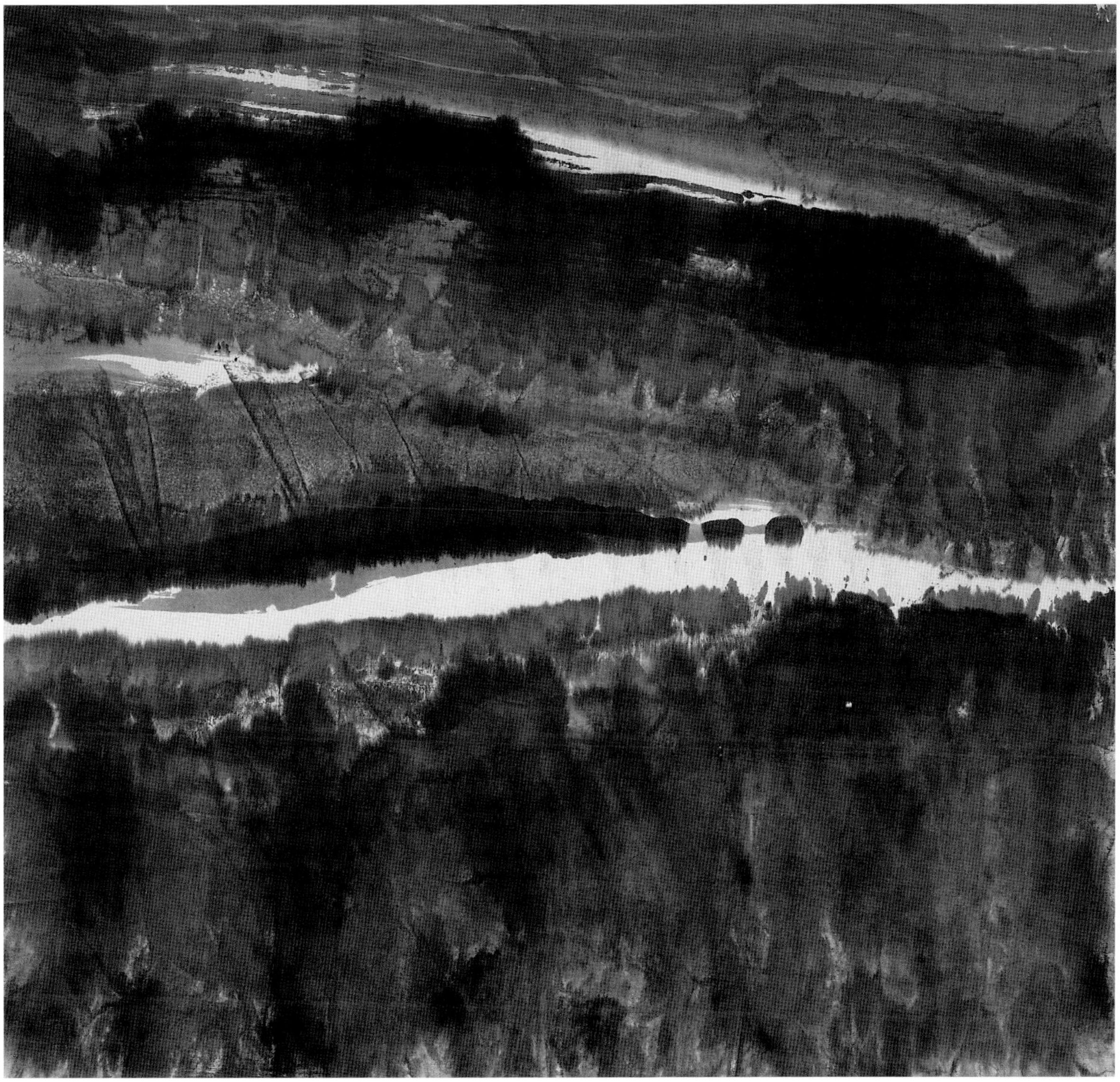

Primeval Forest, 1988, 40.55 x 41.70 in

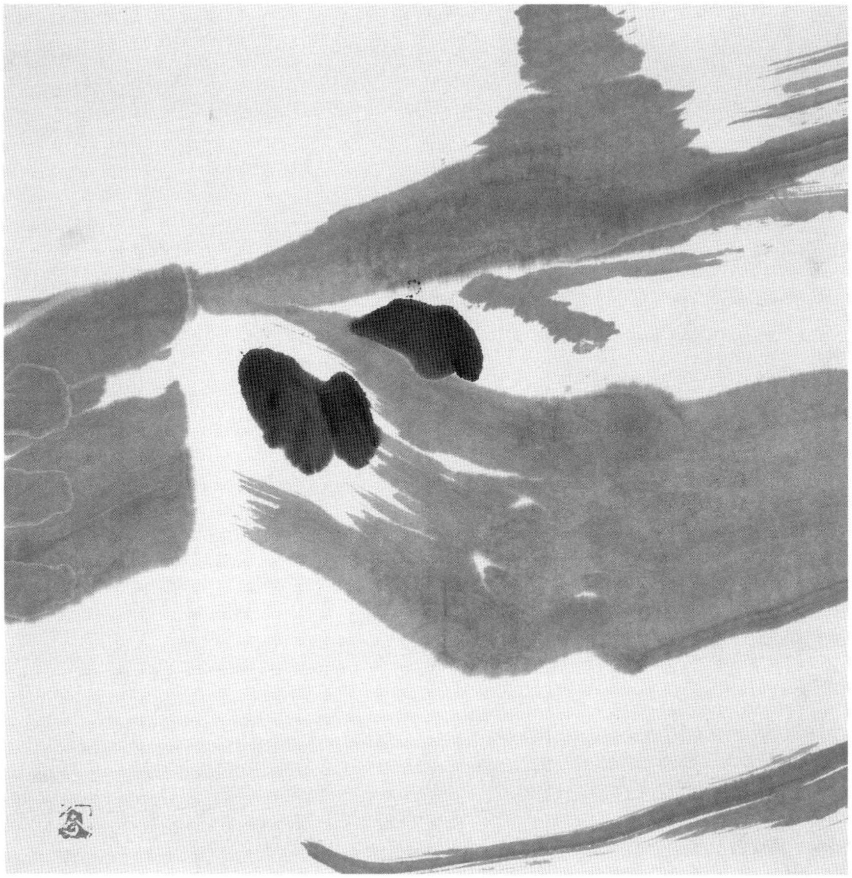

Untitled II, 1988, 15.20 x 14.60 in

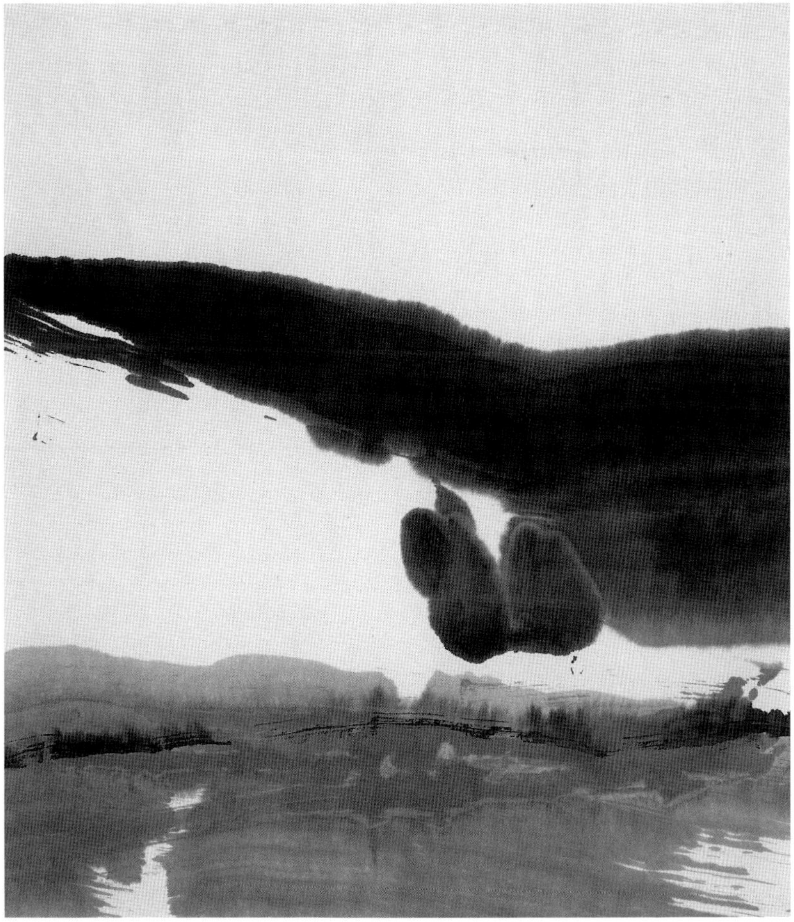

Untitled I, 1988, 16.50 x 14.25 in

A Dream, 1988, 20.90 x 19.80 in

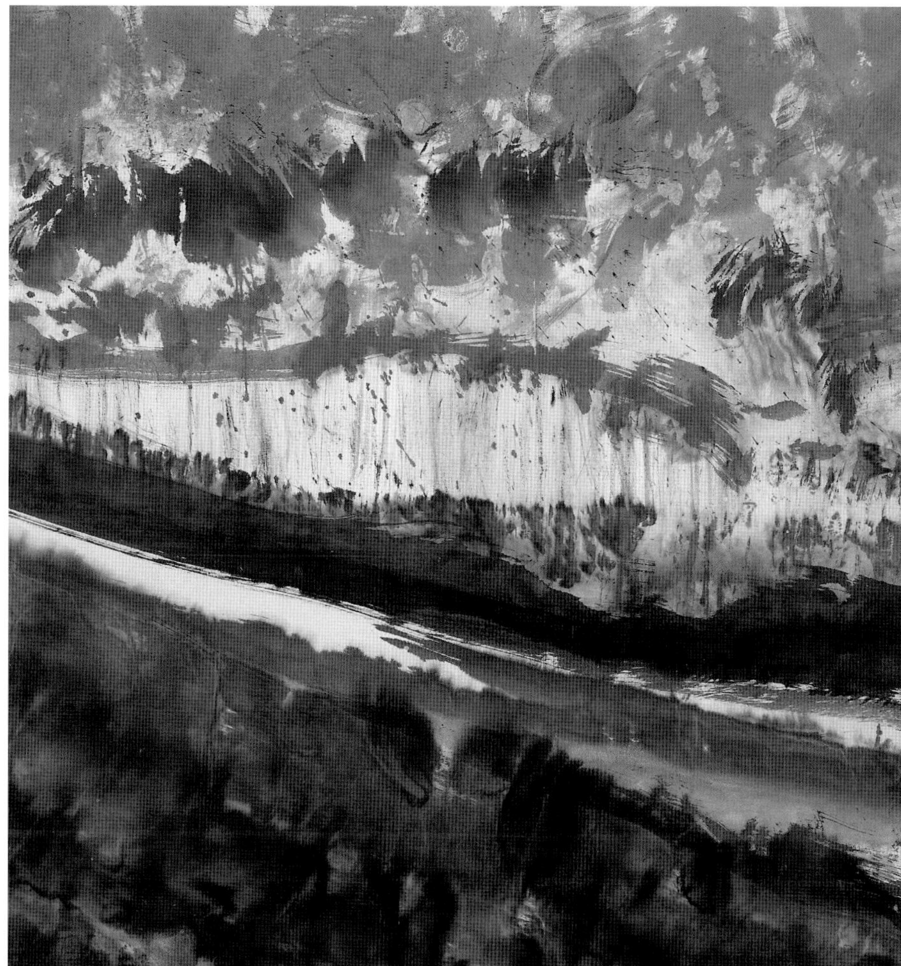

Black Flowers, 1988, 33 x 30.35 in

The Nostalgia, 1988, 104.30 x 64.80 in, on canvas

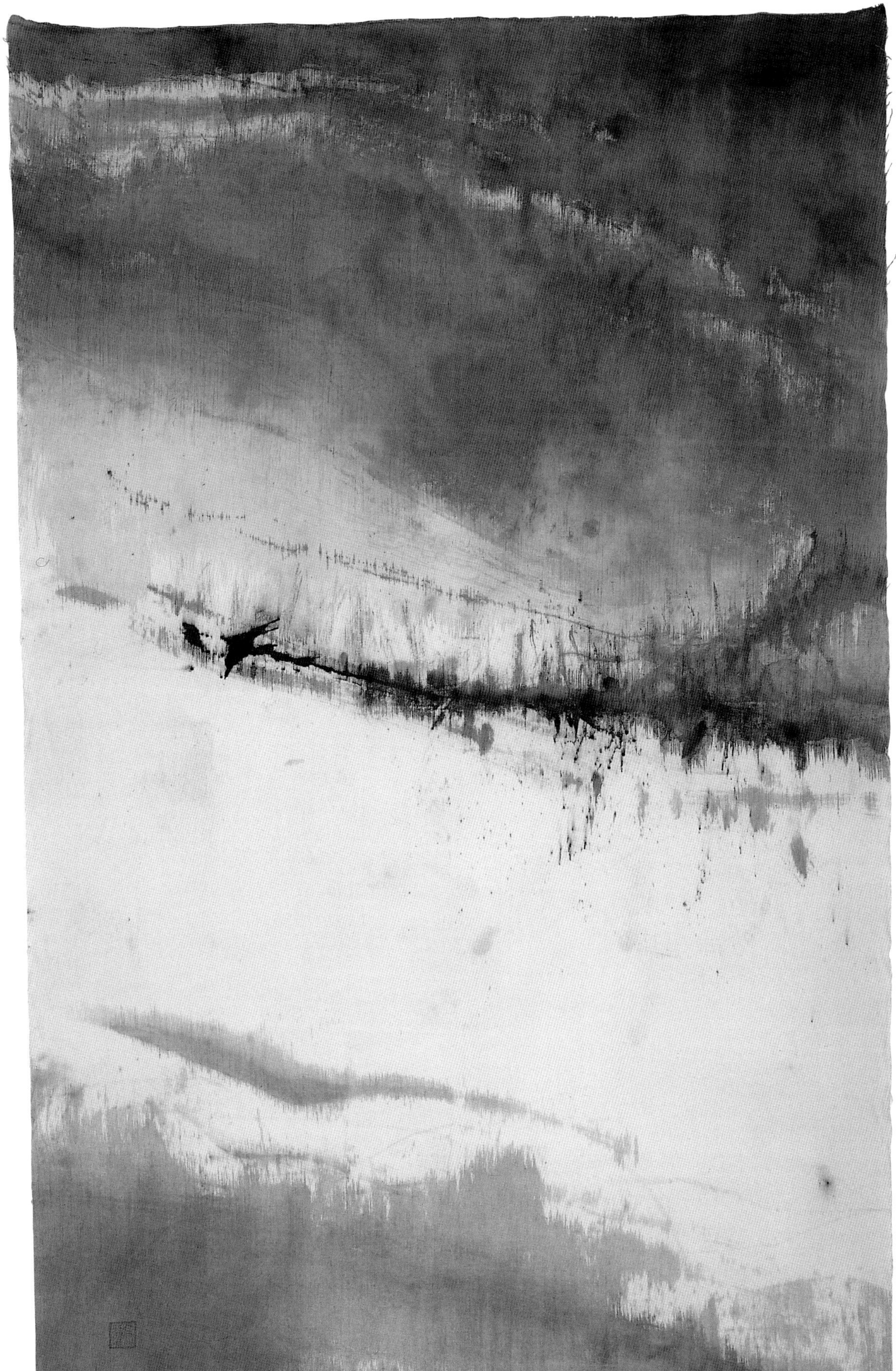

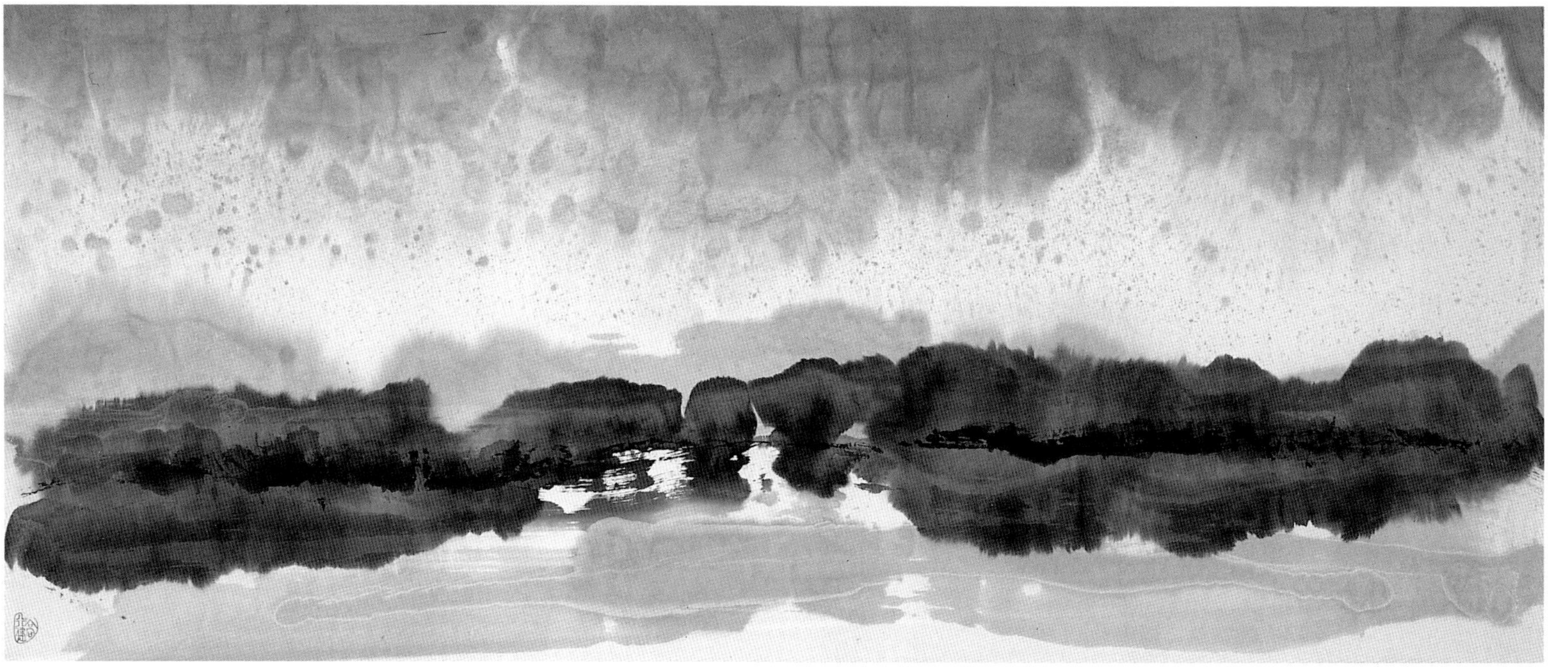

 Early Spring River, 1988, 30.70 x 69.60 in

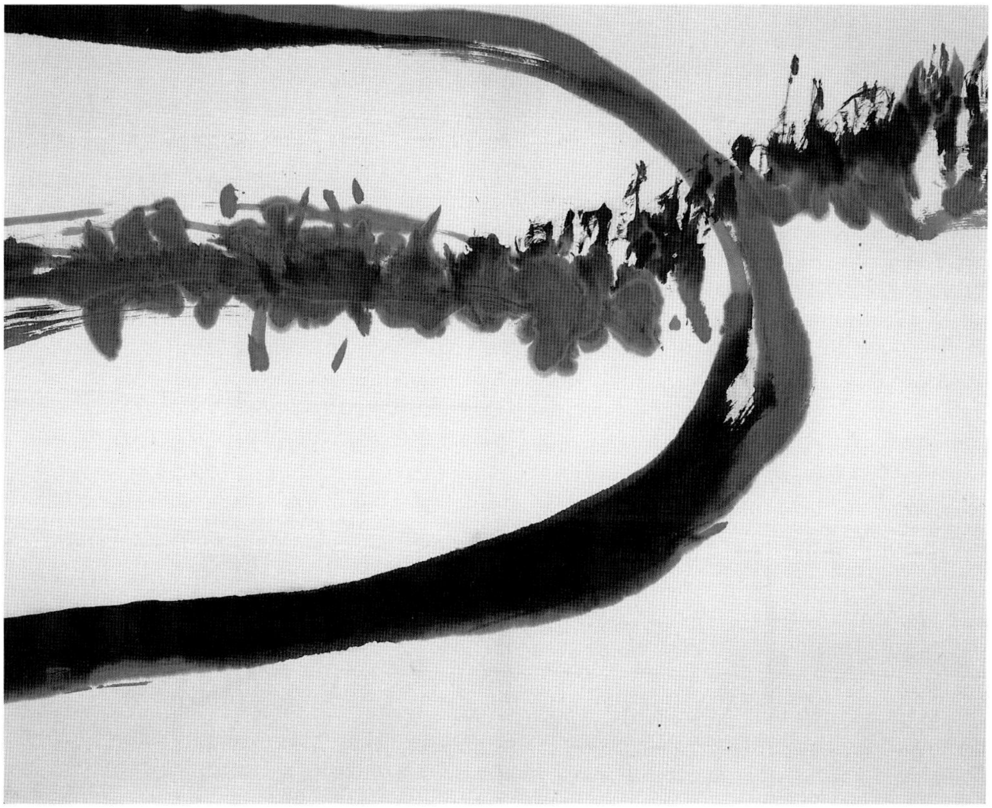

One Goes to War, 1988, 32.40 x 39.65 in

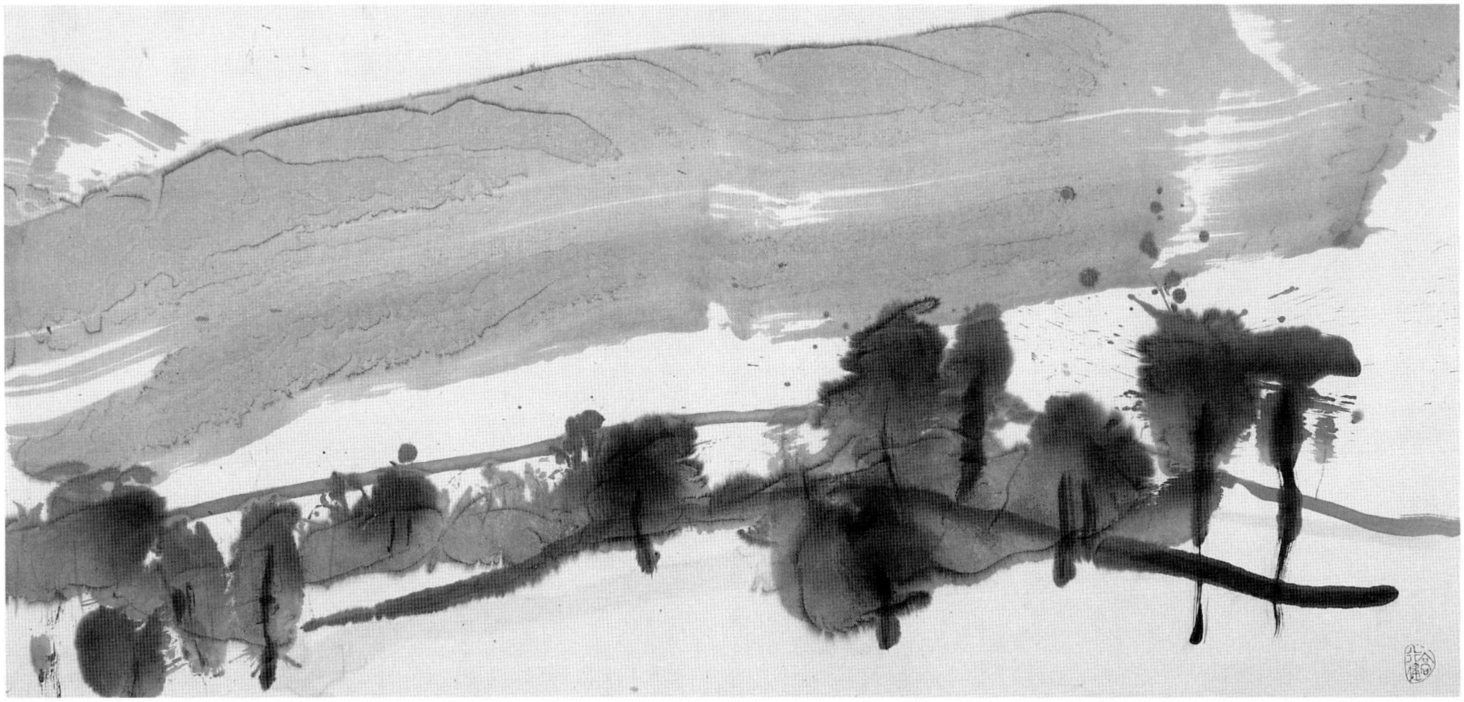

A Cursive Landscape, 1988, 26.20 x 52.80 in

One Afternoon, 1989, 27 x 20.70 in

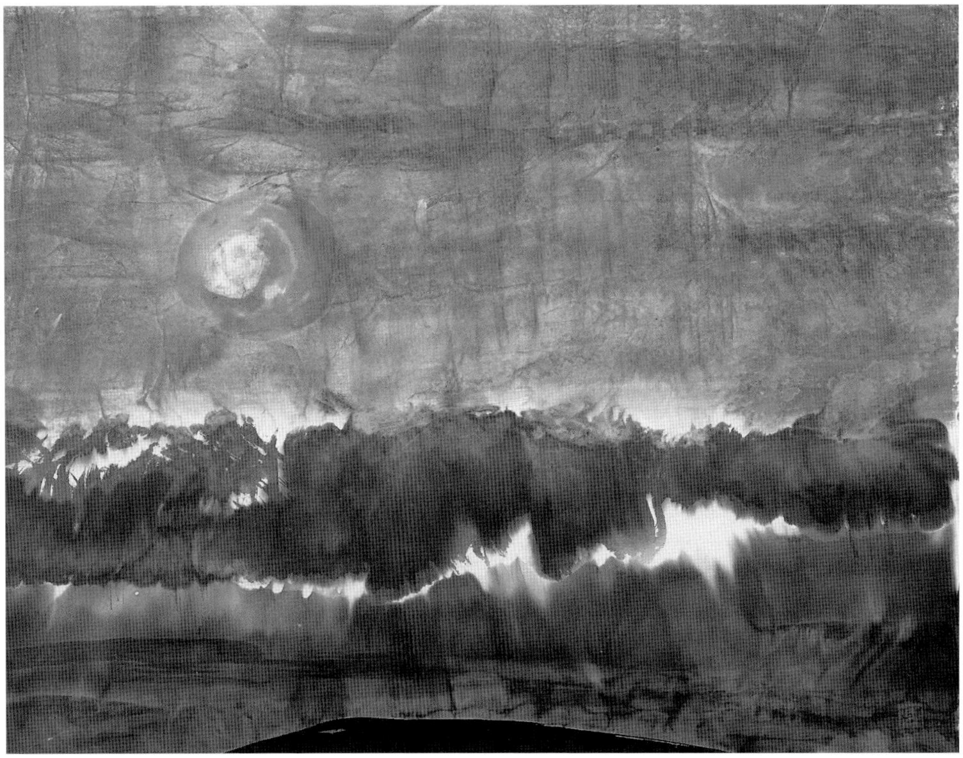

Sketch of the Night, 1989, 28.35 x 35.40 in

Sky and Supersky, 1989, 124 x 55.95 in

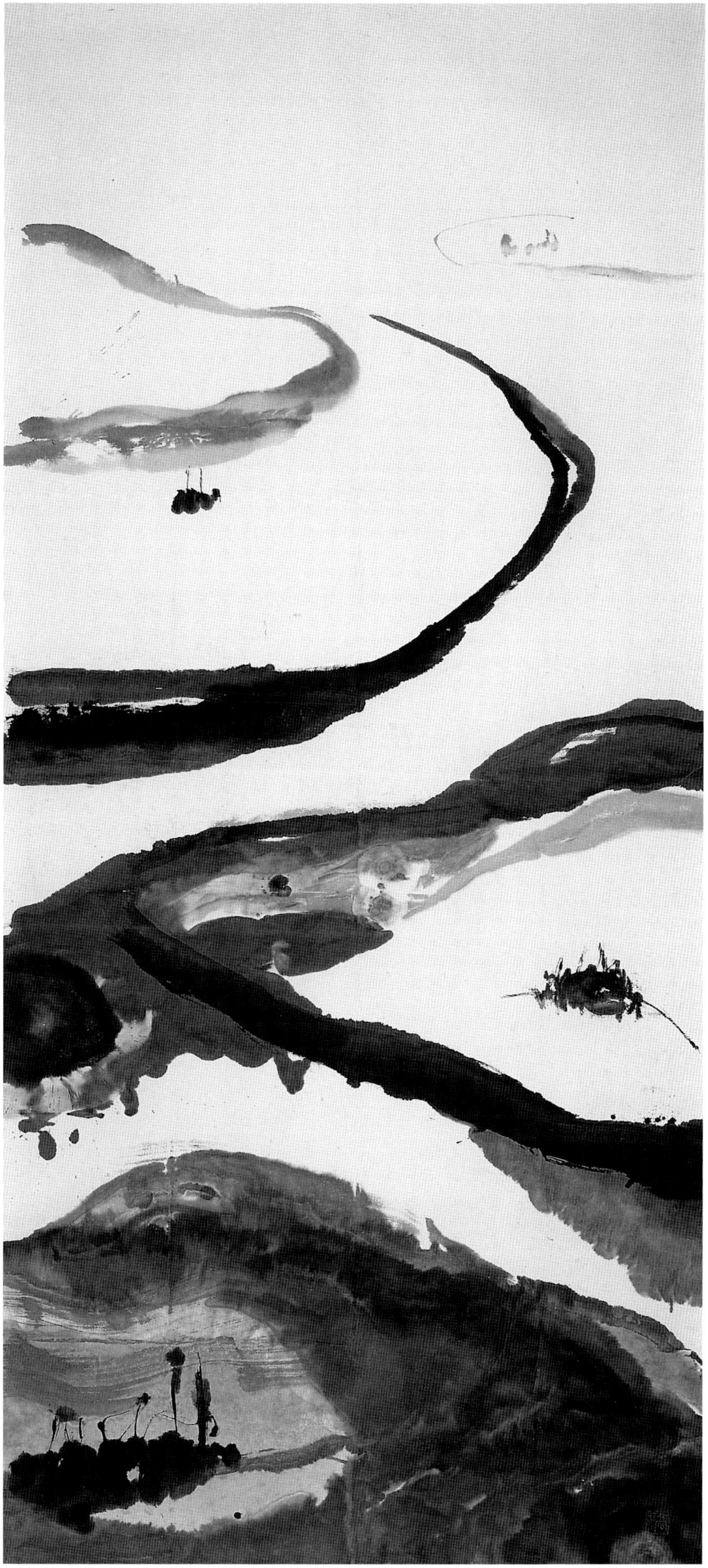

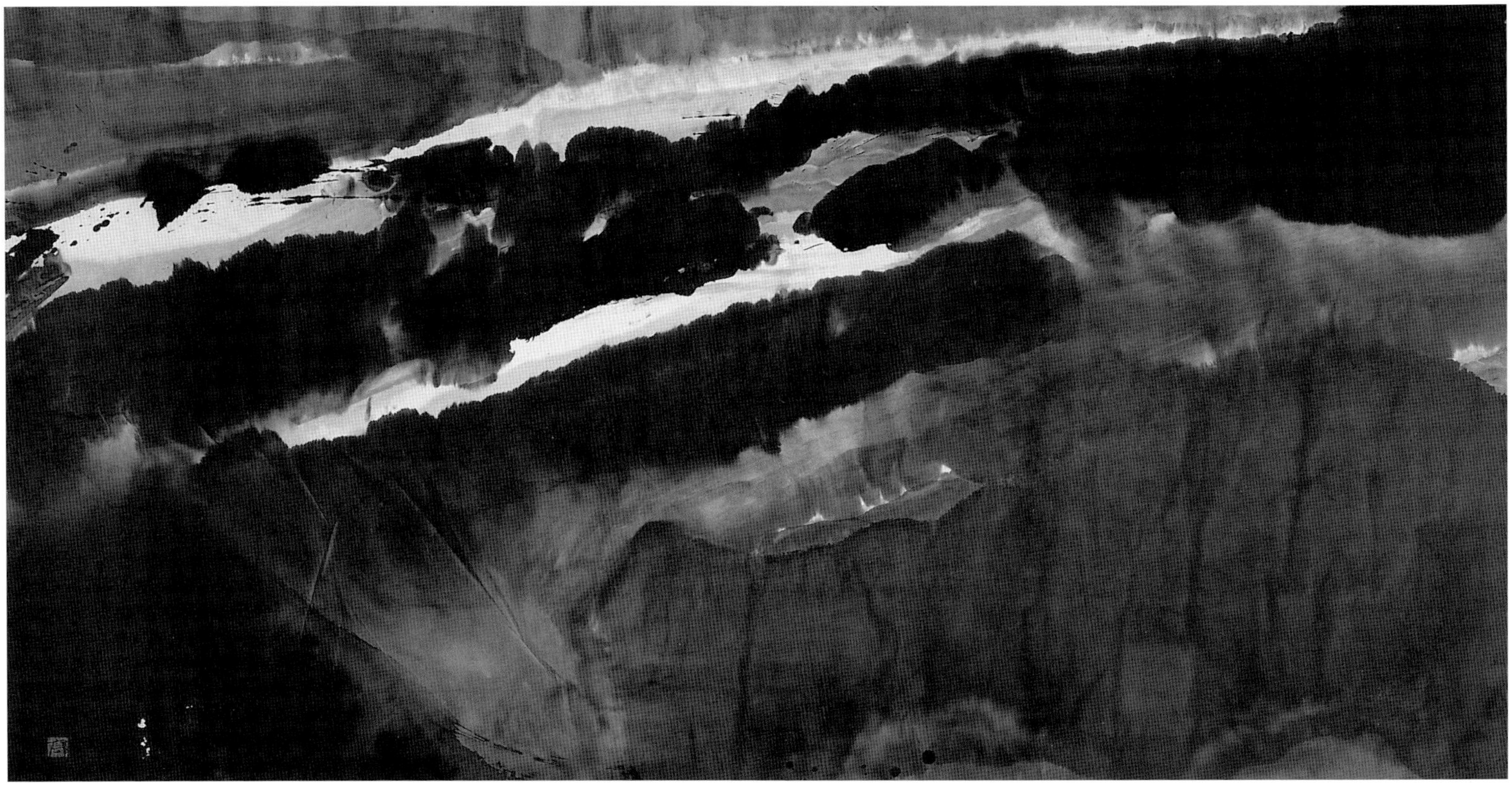

 The River of Forget, 1989, 37.40 x 70.20 in

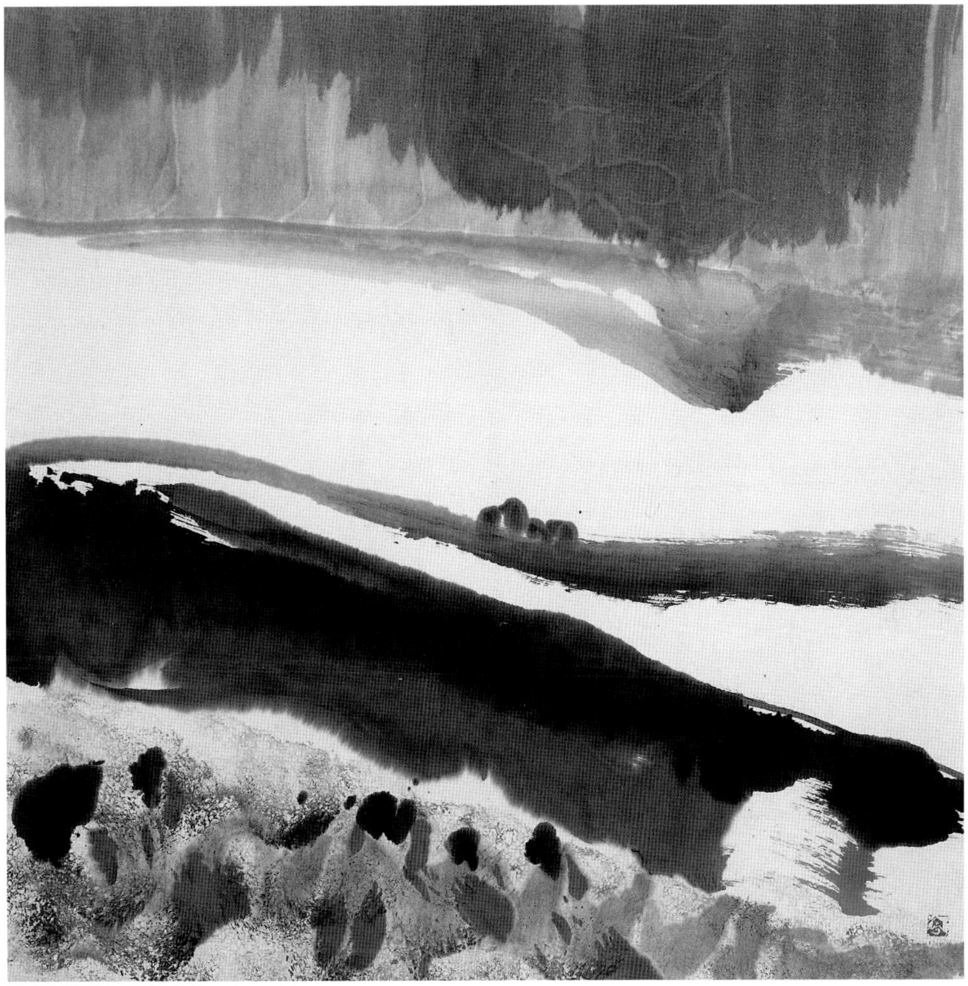

Place Without Human Trace, 1989, 27.90 x 27 in

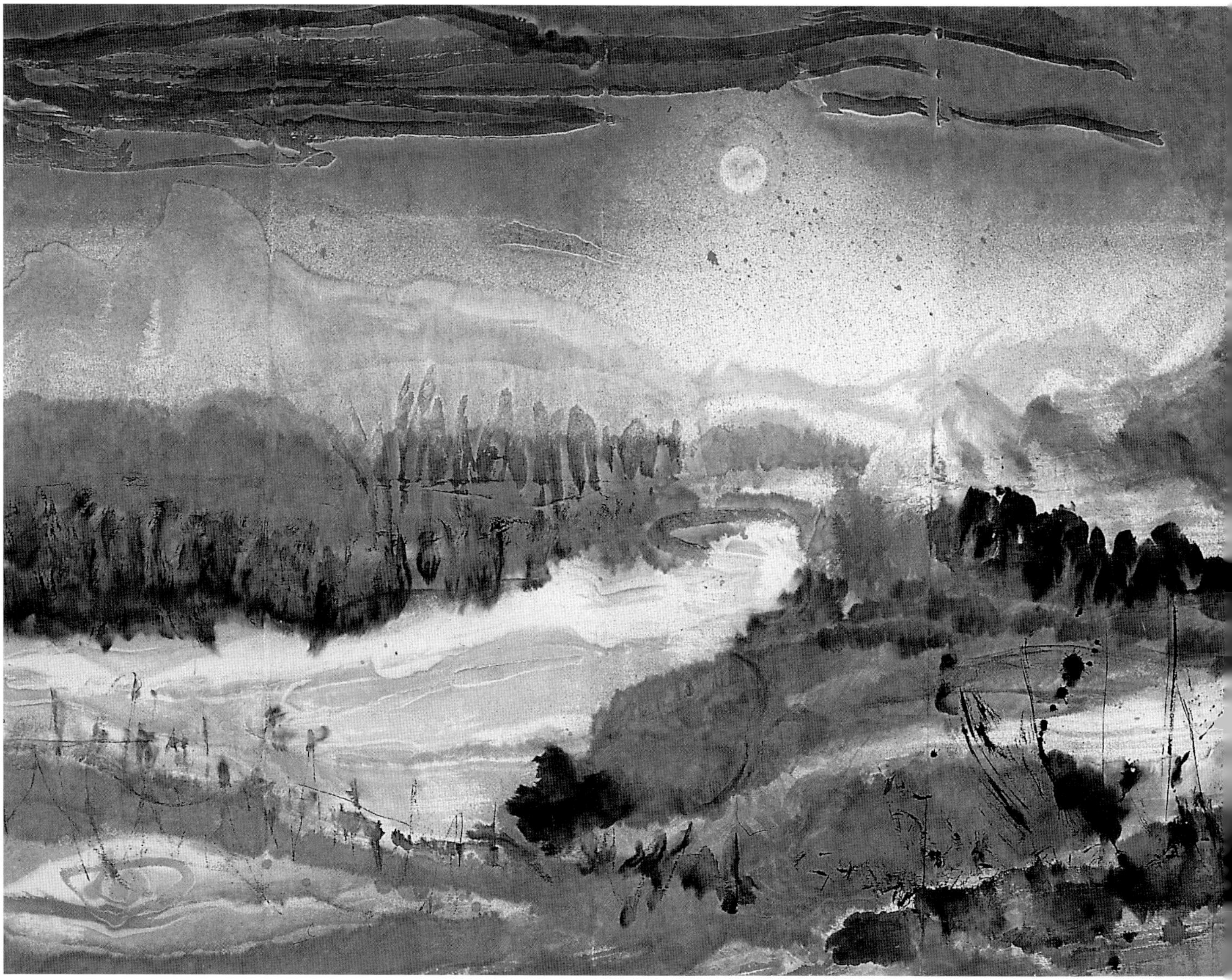

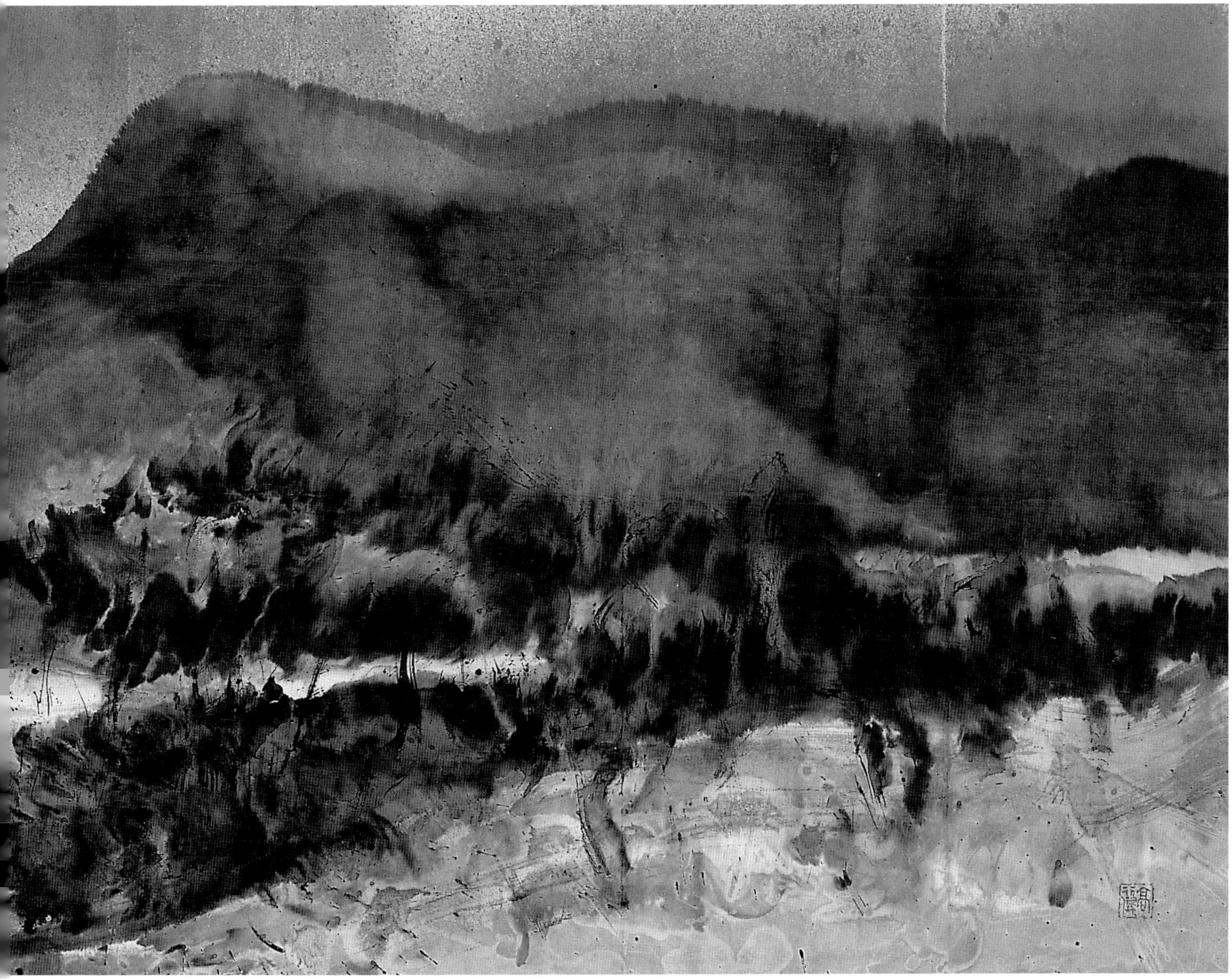

Moonlight, 1989, 54.60 x 138.20 in

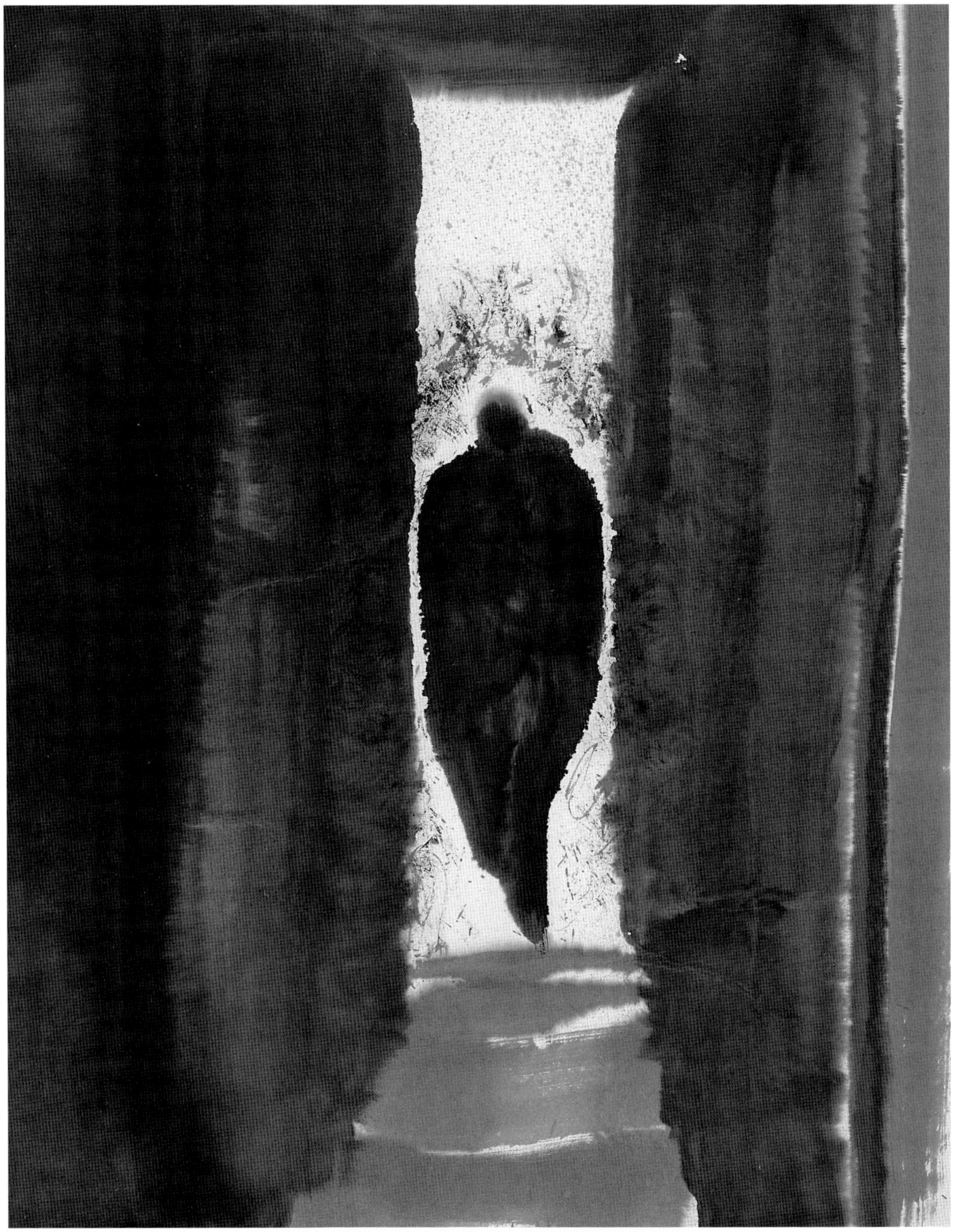

Illusion, 1989, 50 x 38.20 in

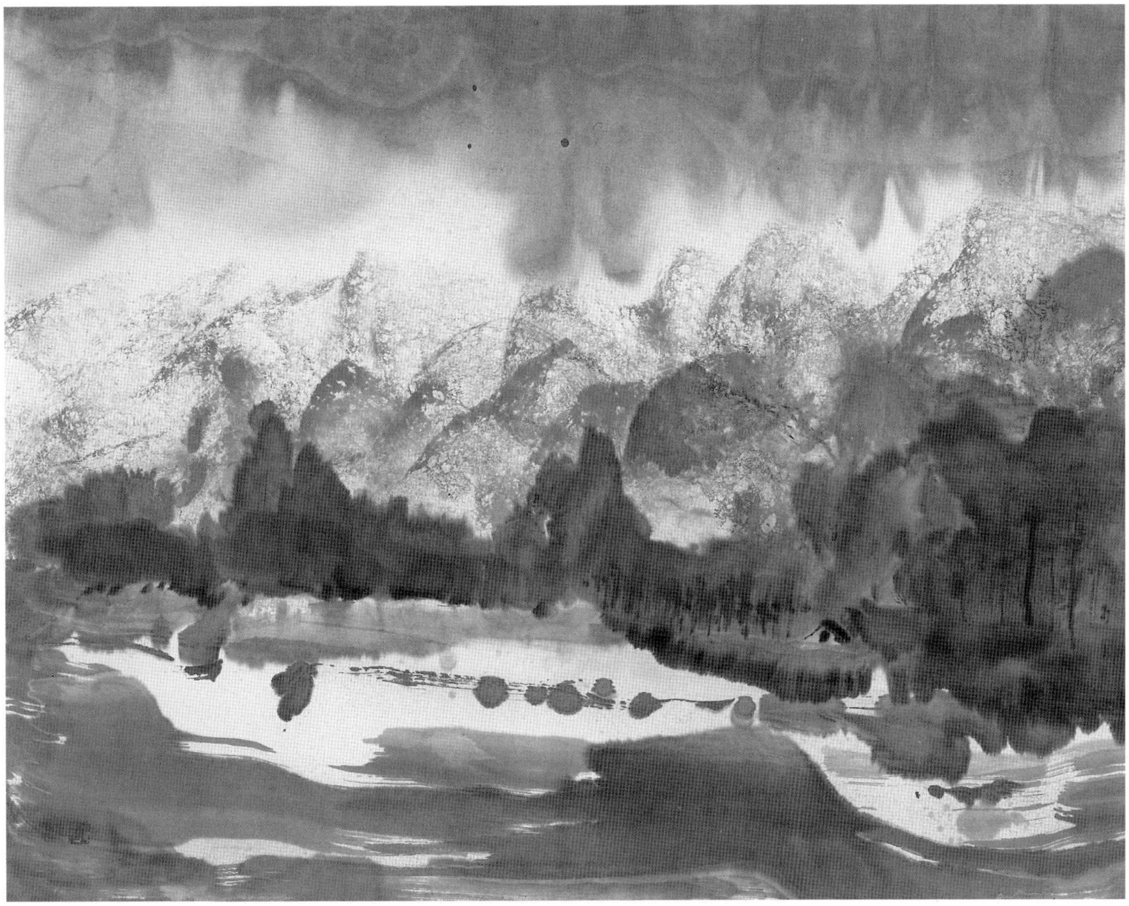

Hermitage, 1990, 26.30 x 32.70 in

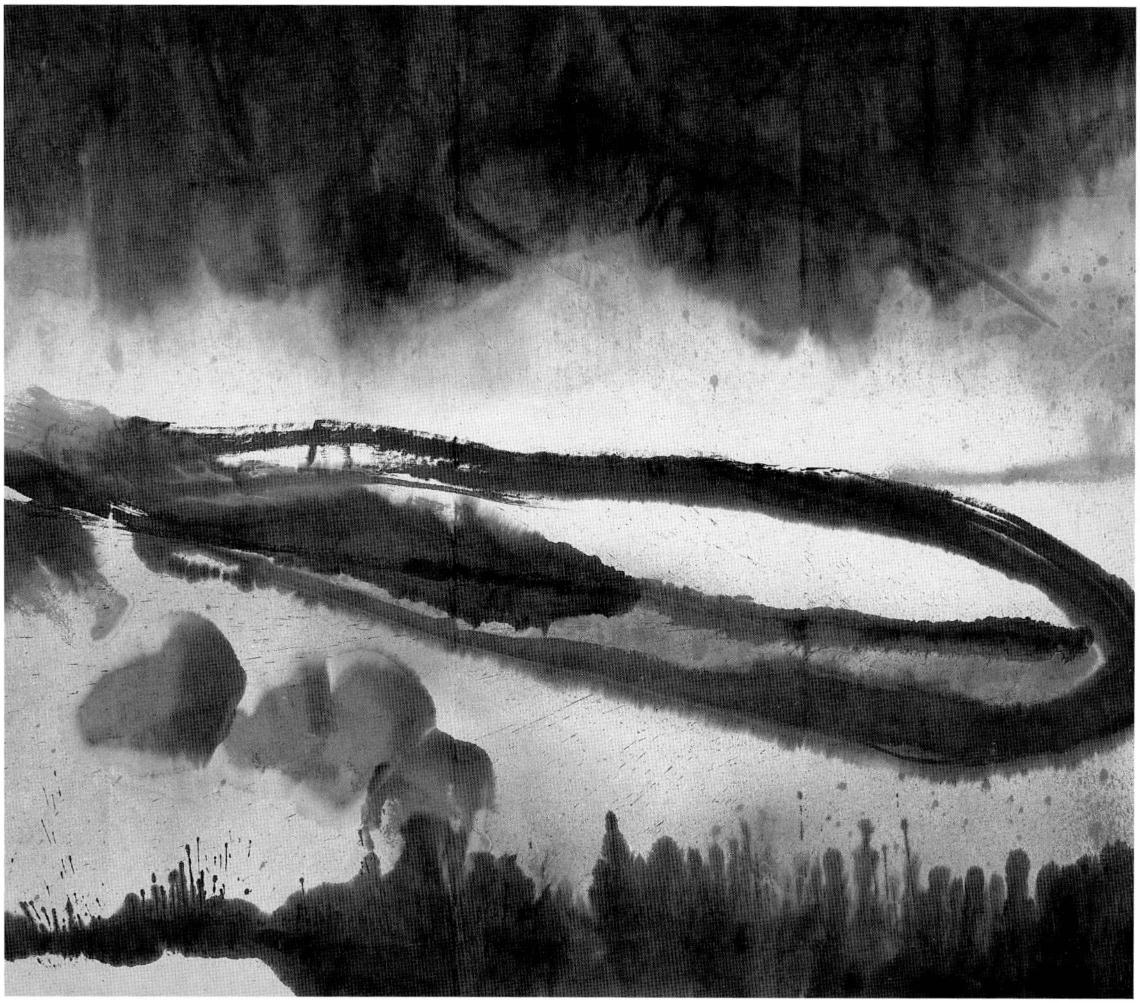

Under the Rain, 1990, 53.90 x 60.20 in

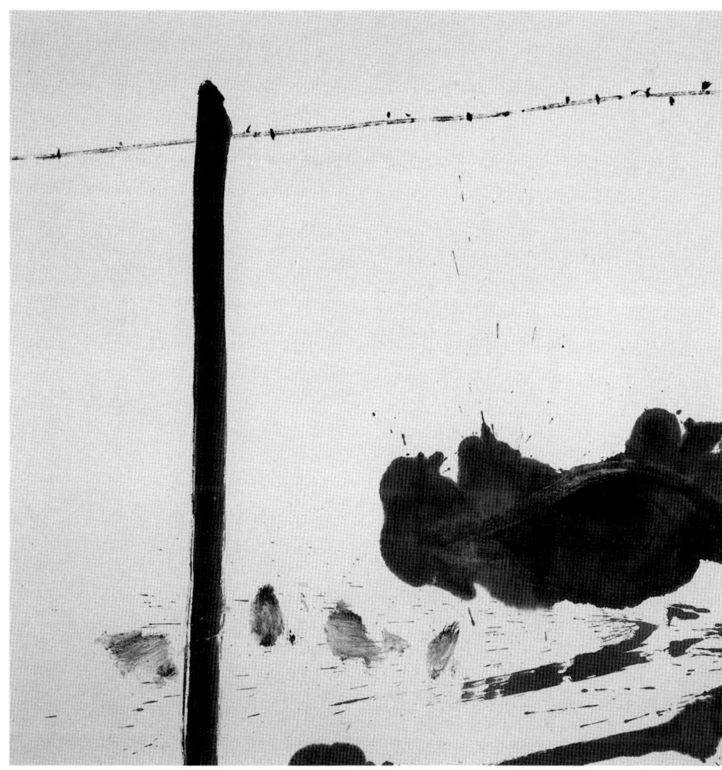

Birds and Lines, 1990, 29.30 x 28.20 in

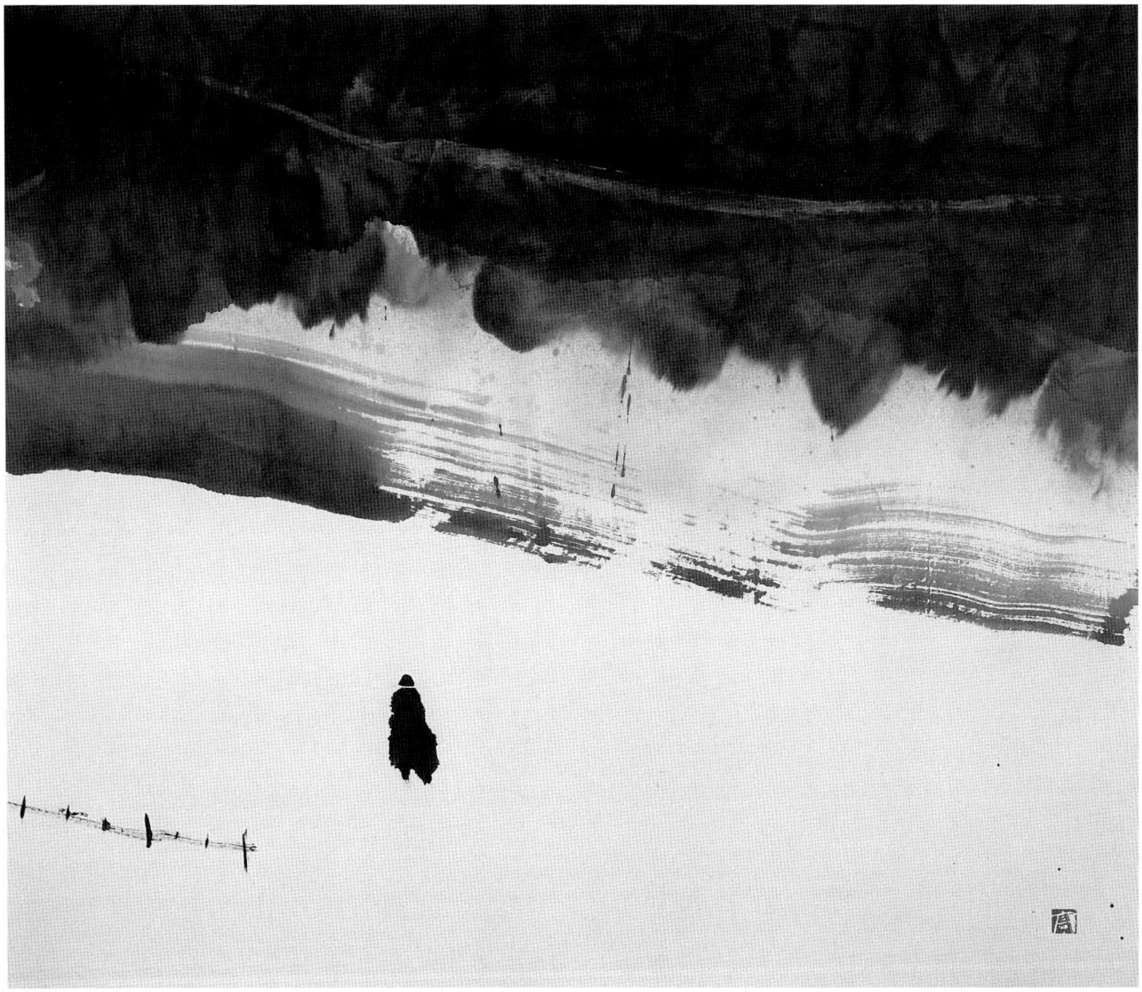

 The Fate, 1991, 37.30 x 42.60 in

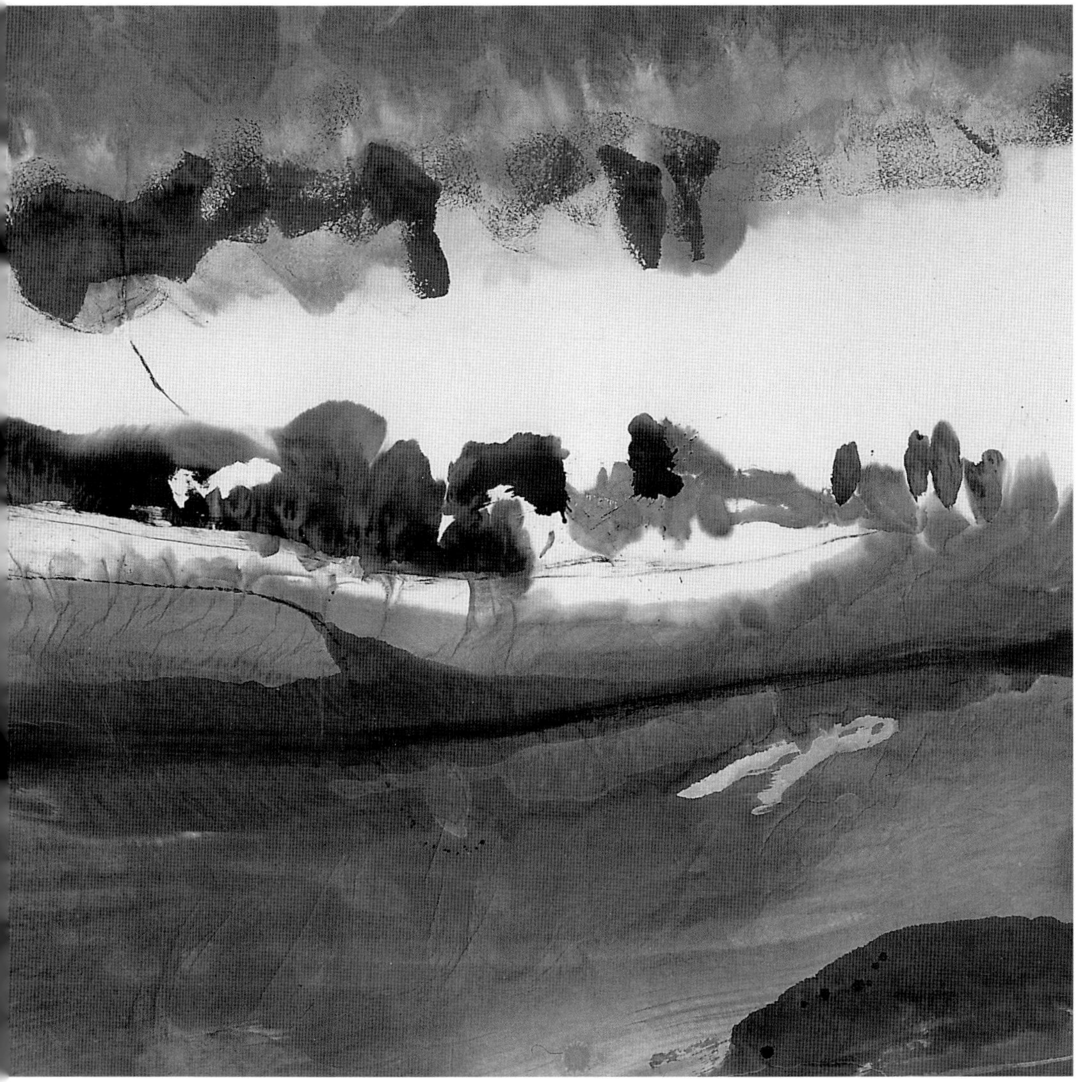

Under the Snow, 1992, 48.80 x 97.60 in

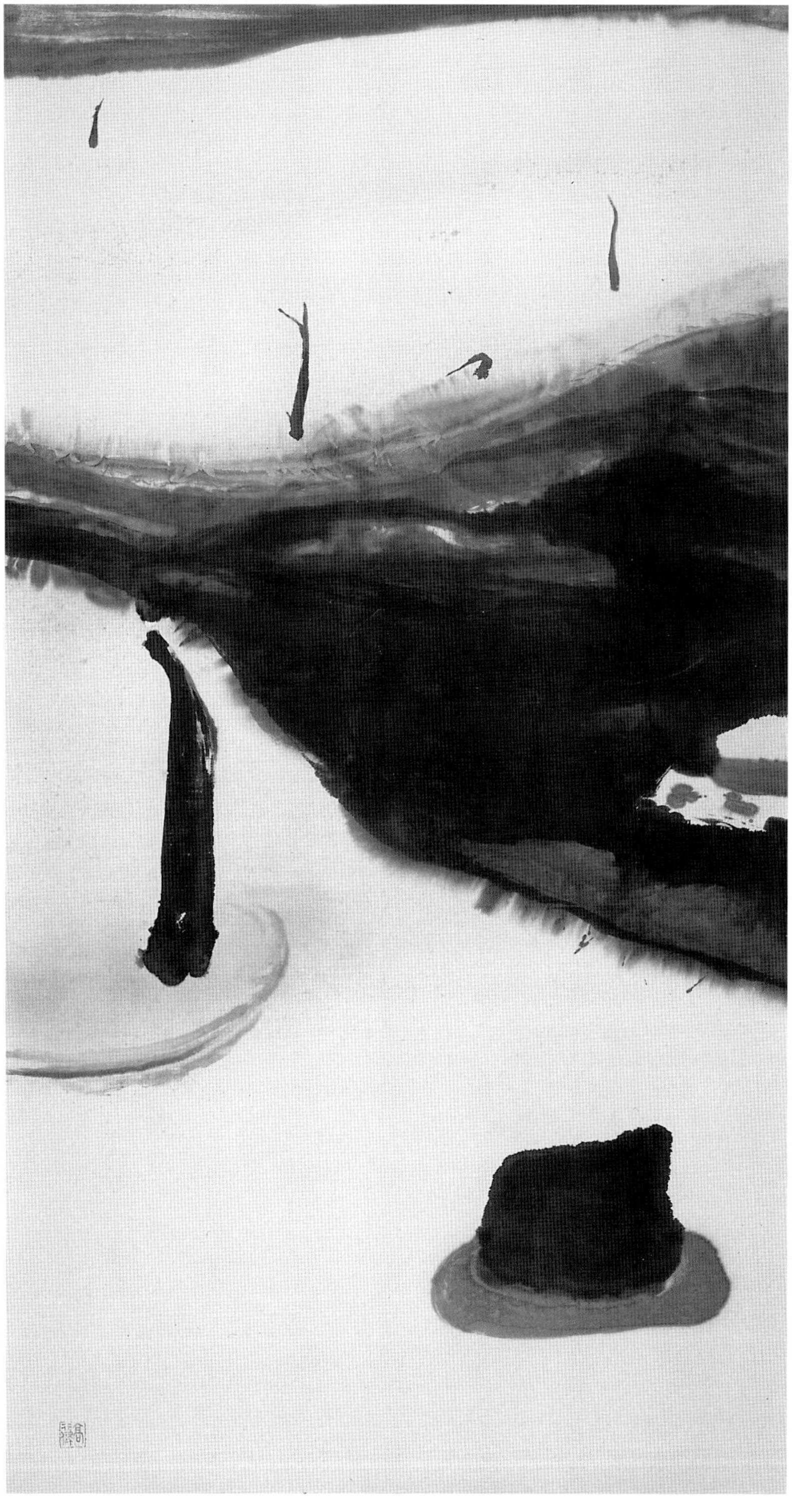

 Enigma, 1992, 108.30 x 57.10 in

List of Works by Gao Xingjian at the Morat Collection:

1. The Soul of the Tree, 1983, 40.20 x 20.80 inches, Page 18
2. The Improvisation, 1983, 31.80 x 26.60 inches, Page 19
3. Woodcut Effect, 1983, 17.60 x 25.20 inches, Page 20
4. Sacrifice I, 1983, 26.10 x 25.20 inches, Page 21
5. Inner Visions I, 18.50 x 16.95 inches
6. The Magic Mountain, 1983, 40.20 x 40.55 inches, Page 22
7. Untitled, 1985, 19.60 x 32.20 inches, Page 23
8. Emotion, 1985, 26.65 x 34.95 inches, Page 24
9. Forest of Rocks, 1985, 27 x 53.70 inches, Page 25
10. Before the Troubles, 1985, 26.90 x 53.60 inches
11. The Winter Fog, 1985, 26.60 x 30.10 inches
12. Italic Writing, 1985, 26.90 x 53.60 inches, Page 26
13. A Black Game, 1985, 41.10 x 40 inches, Page 27
14. The Creation of the World, 1985, 38.35 x 83.10 inches, Page 28
15. Inner Vision III, 1985, 21.30 x 26.80 inches
16. The Taste of Inc II, 1985, 39.80 x 40.55 inches, Page 29
17. The Taste of Inc IV, 1985, 39.80 x 40.55 inches, Page 30
18. The Taste of Inc V, 1985, 40.95 x 40.55 inches, Page 31
19. This Bank, 1985, 53.50 x 26.80 inches, Page 32
20. The Other Bank, 1985, 53.50 x 26.80 inches, Page 33
21. Untitled, 1985, 26.40 x 26.40 inches, Page 34
22. Birth, 1985, 37.80 x 80.70 inches, Page 35
23. The Desire, 1986, 26.40 x 53.60 inches, Page 38
24. Taste of Inc, 1986, 41.10 x 90.20 inches, Pages 36/37
25. Untitled, 1986, 41.10 x 69.70 inches, Page 39
26. River in the Dark, 1986, 22.90 x 37.10 inches, Page 41
27. Prehistoric Legend, 1986, 26 x 39.70 inches, Page 40
28. Anxiousness, 1986, 33.10 x 59.65 inches, Pages 44/45
29. The Moon, 1986, 26.80 x 26.60 inches, Page 42
30. The Dancer, 1986, 16.90 x 11.65 inches, Page 8
31. Scroll II (Untitled), 1986, 22.20 x 24.30 inches, Page 8
32. A Sitting Man, 1986, 15.55 x 11.70 inches, Page 43
33. Between Sky and Earth, 1987, 48.80 x 97.05 inches, Pages 46/47
34. In the Heart of the Mountain, 1987, 12.80 x 15.50 inches, Page 50
35. A Flower, 1987, 13.80 x 12.20 inches, Page 48
36. Two Women, 1987, 19.10 x 18.20 inches, Page 52
37. The Horizon, 1987, 35.70 x 39.45 inches, Page 49
38. The Dead Season, 1987, 35.90 x 33.30 inches, Page 51
39. Ravine, 1988, 25.75 x 52.80 inches
40. Vineyard, 1988, 34.65 x 33.70 inches
41. Dry River, 1988, 38.50 x 39 inches
42. Sanddune, 1988, 39.70 x 38.60 inches
43. Early Spring, 1988, 37.20 x 68.40 inches
44. A Dream, 1988, 20.90 x 19.80 inches, Page 56
45. The Cursive Landscape, 1988, 26.85 x 52.60 inches
46. Primeval Forest, 1988, 40.55 x 41.70 inches, Page 53
47. Untitled I, 1988, 16.50 x 14.25 inches, Page 55
48. Untitled II, 1988, 15.20 x 14.60 inches, Page 54
49. Solar Eclipse, 1988, 15.60 x 15 inches
50. On the Beach, 1988, 25.60 x 21.30 inches

51. One Goes to War, 1988, 32.40 x 39.65 inches, Page 61
52. Black Flowers, 1988, 33 x 30.35 inches, Page 57
53. The Nostalgia, 1988, 104.30 x 64.80 inches, On Canvas, Page 56
54. Early Spring River, 1988, 30.70 x 69.60 inches, Page 60
55. A Cursive Landscape, 1988, 26.20 x 52.80 inches, Page 62
56. Under the Snow, 1989, 26.70 x 53.40 inches
57. One Afternoon, 1989, 27 x 20.70 inches, Page 63
58. Sketch of the Night, 1989, 28.35 x 35.40 inches, Page 64
59. Place Without Human Trace, 1989, 27.90 x 27 inches, Page 67
60. Ideogram, 1989, 37.40 x 70.20 inches
61. Crack, 1989, 37.20 x 70.30 inches
62. After the Thunderstorm, 1989, 37.40 x 70.20 inches
63. The River of Forget, 1989, 37.40 x 70.20 inches, Page 66
64. Illusion, 1989, 50 x 38.20 inches, Page 70
65. Sleeping Village, 1989, 27 x 54.10 inches
66. Sky and Supersky, 1989, 124 x 55.95 inches, Page 65
67. Moonlight, 1989, 54.60 x 138.20 inches, Pages 68/69
68. Dead Village, 1990, 52.05 x 71.65 inches
69. Revelation, 1990, 32.90 x 36.80 inches
70. The White House, 1990, 32.90 x 36.80 inches
71. Spring Flood, 1990, 19.70 x 15.75 inches
72. Legend of the Childhood, 1990, 32.90 x 33.35 inches
73. Mountain Soul, 1990, 53.50 x 70.40 inches
74. Under the Rain, 1990, 53.90 x 60.20 inches, Page 72
75. The Winter, 1990, 52 x 69.10 inches
76. Hermitage, 1990, 26.30 x 32.70 inches, Page 71
77. Birds and Lines, 1990, 29.30 x 28.20 inches, Page 73
78. White Night, 1991, 26.70 x 36 inches
79. The Fate, 1991, 37.30 x 42.60 inches, Page 74
80. Wind on a High Plateau, 1991, 38.10 x 32.30 inches, Page 75
81. Sacrifice II, 1991, 26.70 x 53.90 inches
82. Untitled, 1991, 32.90 x 31.70 inches, Page 76
83. The Snow, 1991, 32.80 x 59.60 inches, Page 77
84. Springtime, 1991, 32.95 x 59.80 inches
85. Autumn, 1991, 32.50 x 59.70 inches
86. Untitled, 1991, 18.30 x 16.90 inches
87. Dead Town, 1991, 32.80 x 58.10 inches
88. Interior Landscape, 1991, 60.10 x 32.30 inches
89. Meditation I, 1991, 56.60 x 44.80 inches
90. Surprise I, 1991, 73.50 x 48.20 inches
91. Meditation II, 1991, 81.20 x 56.85 inches, Page 78
92. Sacrifice, 1992, 106.70 x 65.70 inches
93. Surprise II, 1992, 106.70 x 65.70 inches, Page 79
94. Under the Snow, 1992, 48.80 x 97.60 inches, Pages 80/81
95. Enigma, 1992, 108.30 x 57.10 inches, Page 82
96. Dreamland, 1992, 33.10 x 27.60 inches, Page 83
97. The Legends, 1992, 48.80 x 97.60 inches
98. The Revelation, 1992, 48.80 x 57.10 inches
99. Towards the Unknown, 1993, 48.80 x 97.60 inches, Page 85
100. Elegance, 1993, 48.80 x 98 inches
101. Nostalgia, 1993, 48.80 x 43.30 inches
102. Untitled, 1993, 56.50 x 70.30 inches

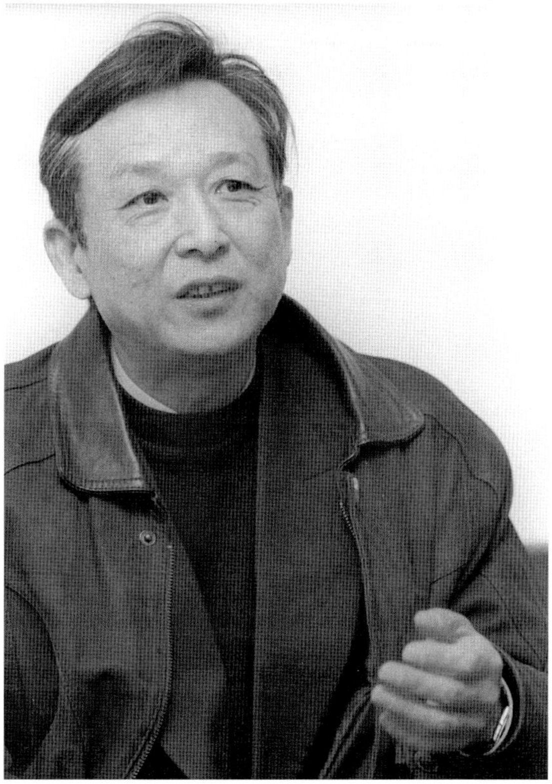

Gao Xingjian, born in 1940 in China. Lives and works in Paris.

Solo Exhibitions

1985 Theater of People's Art, Beijing
1985 Künstlerhaus Bethanien, Berlin
1985 Alte Schmiede, Vienna, Austria
1987 Cultural Department, Lille, France
1988 Community Office of Fine Arts and Culture, Watterlos, France
1989 Östasiatiska Museet, Malmö, Sweden
1989 Krapperrus Konsthall, Malmö, Sweden
1990 Centre Culturel de Lumière de Chine, Marseilles, France
1991 Contemporary Art Space Confluence, Rambouillet, France
1992 Contemporary Art Space le Cercle Bleu, Metz, France
1992 Asian Cultural Center, Marseilles, France
1993 House of Culture of Bourges, Bourges, France
1993 Art Gallery la Tour des Cardineaux, Isle-sur-la-Sorgue, France
1993 Hexagon Gallery, Aachen, Germany
1994 Contemporary Art Space le Cercle Bleu, Metz, France
1994 Polish Theater, Poznan, Poland
1995 Taipei Fine Arts Museum, Taiwan
1996 Palais de la Justice, Luxembourg
1996 Contemporary Art Space le Cercle Bleu, Metz, France
1996 Art Gallery la Tour des Cardineaux, Isle-sur-la-Sorgue, France
1996 Alisan Fine Arts, Hong Kong
1997 The Gallery Schimmel Center for the Arts, New York
1998 Art Gallery la Tour des Cardineaux, Isle-sur-la-Sorgue, France

1998 Contemporary Art Space le Cercle Bleu, Metz, France
1998 4 Arts, Cean, France
1998 Alisan Fine Arts, Hong Kong
1999 Le Printemps Du Livre, Cassis, France
1999 Art Gallery la Tour des Cardineaux, Isle-sur-la-Sorgue, France
1999 Boulevard des Potes, Bordeaux, France
1999 Scène National de Bayonne, Bayonne, France
2000 Asiart Center, Taipei
2001 Palais des Papes, Avignon, France

Group Exhibitions

1989 The Gallery Michael Goedhuis, London
1989 Grand Palais, Figuration Critique, Paris
1990 Grand Palais, Figuration Critique, Paris
1991 Grand Palais, Figuration Critique, Paris
1991 Trejiakov Gallery, Figuration Critique, Moscow
1998 XIXth International Biennale of Antiques Sellers, Carrousel Du Louvre, Paris
2000 Art Paris, Carrousel du Louvre, Paris

Works in Public Collections

Morat Institute of Art and Science of Art, Freiburg I. Br., Germany
Leibniz Company for Cultural Exchange, Berlin
Östasiatiska Museet, Stockholm, Sweden
Museum of Modern Art, Stockholm
Krapperrus Konsthall, Malmö, Sweden
House of Culture of Bourges, Bourges, France
Artothèque, Nantes, France
Taipei Fine Arts Museum, Taiwan
Théâtre Molière, Paris